Why Cleaning has Meaning

Why Cleaning has Meaning

Bringing Wellbeing Into Your Home

Linda Thomas

Floris Books

First published in English in 2014 by Floris Books
The author originally wrote the book in German, published
in 2011 under the title *Putzen!? Von der lästigen Notwendigkeit
zu einer Liebeserklärung an die Gegenwart* by
Verlag am Goetheanum, Dornach, Switzerland

 This book is also available as an eBook

British Library CIP Data available

ISBN 978-178250-050-6

Printed in Poland

Contents

1. How I Came into Cleaning and Caring

South Africa to Switzerland

*Until one is committed, there is hesitancy, the chance to draw
back, always ineffectiveness. Concerning all acts of initiative
(and creation), there is one elementary truth that ignorance of
which kills countless ideas and splendid plans: that the moment
one definitely commits oneself, then Providence moves too.
All sorts of things occur to help one that would never otherwise
have occurred. A whole stream of events issues from the decision,
raising in one's favor all manner of unforeseen incidents and
meetings and material assistance, which no man could have
dreamt would have come his way. I learned a deep respect for one
of Goethe's couplets: 'Whatever you can do or dream you can,
begin it. Boldness has genius, power, and magic in it.'*

William Hutchison Murray (1913–96)[1]

Years before I even thought of writing a book, I found this quote on a
desk in a house I was cleaning. It moved me because it confirmed so
much of what had happened in my life. The very person whose house
I was busy cleaning was a woman who has had a profound influence
in my life. Because of her, I was offered the possibility of cleaning the
Goetheanum. She was the one who organised the first interview that
was ever published on my work. Through her, providence has moved
many times in my life.

But let me start at the beginning. Why did I start cleaning? This
most menial of tasks still fills me with awe, just thinking of the incred-

ible potential it has to change things. Most of what I have learned in life, I learned through my children. Most of the things I have really understood in life came to me through over twenty years of experience as a professional cleaner.

As a young girl, I had one ideal only and that was to become a house-wife and mother: full-time. But as so often in life, destiny took a turn in another direction. I was born in 1953 in a very small village in South Africa as the middle child of seven siblings. We lived in many different places, but what remains most strongly in my memory is a smallholding in a very poor farming community, where we lived on and off from my fourth until my fourteenth year.

I often heard children talking about only primitive people having such large families. When confronting my father with this, he simply replied, 'Primitive people do not look after themselves and their sur-roundings, they live in dirt, and no longer have any dignity or sense of human values.' This reply made a deep impression on me.

As we were very poor, my father taught us that the only capital we possessed and could rely on, was our intelligence, ability and willing-ness to work. It became very clear that there would never be any money for studies and that those of us who wished to go to the university would have to obtain a scholarship through our own diligence.

We lived off the land and we all learned to help at a very tender age. We learned to plant and care for vegetables, we could harvest and pro-cess fruit, cook, bake, sew and mend our own clothes – yet we never learned how to clean. We neither had to make our own beds, nor clean our own shoes. For during the apartheid era even the poorest of white people had servants, as the black people were often even poorer than we were. At fourteen years of age, I experienced a cultural shock. We moved from our small provincial town to Johannesburg to a big hostile city without nature. In our small community we had all been treated as individuals but now, from one day to the next, we were somehow anonymous, just one among many.

Although all my brothers and sisters worked hard to go to university, I knew that I wanted to be a wife and mother of a large family, prefer-ably on a small farm. I did not require a diploma to do this and there-fore had no interest in further study.

The sad fact that I was unable to find a suitable husband directly after leaving school obliged to look for work. I found a job in a bank. There I met a Swiss man who was to become my future husband. Two days after our wedding in February 1977, we left for Switzerland. Our intention was to stay for one year in order to prepare my husband's emigration so that we could settle in South Africa.

On my very first day in Switzerland, I came across the books by Omraam Mikhaël Aïvanhov (1900–1986), the Bulgarian philosopher and mystic. He was to have a profound influence on my life. Discovering a spiritual teaching was such a liberating experience after the strict, Puritan Dutch Reformed Church I had known in South Africa. I felt the strong conviction that to be able to learn from this great teacher was much more important than going back to South Africa. Now, thirty-five years later, I am still living in Switzerland.

Very soon after arriving in Basle, I met a doctor who was about ten years older than my mother. We became close friends and in many ways she took on a maternal role in my life. I was particularly impressed with her talented son and daughter, then aged fourteen and sixteen. Every time I admired a piece of art, be it a painting, a wooden or clay sculpture, or even the copper baking forms in the kitchen, it was made by either her son or daughter. They also both played musical instruments, and during conversations I was most impressed by their wide general knowledge. I complimented my friend in being such a wonderful mother, having educated her children to be so multi-talented. To this she simply replied, 'Of course I try my best, but I am also much indebted to the school they go to.' They were such wonderful young people that I knew that whatever school it was, there had to be something very special about it.

And this is how I learned about the existence of Waldorf or Rudolf Steiner Schools. After visiting a school bazaar a few weeks later, I was convinced that this would be the only kind of school good enough for my future children who, as it turned out, were in no hurry to come. My daughter was born in 1982 and my son five years later. Ten years after my first encounter with the school, my daughter was ready to go to kindergarten. I told my husband that I would like her to go to the Waldorf kindergarten. He considered this a luxury and was quite happy to send her to a 'good state school,' and said, 'If you want to send her to a private school you'll have to finance it yourself.' He quite underestimated the strength of my conviction.

Cleaning company and crisis

My son was only a few months old at the time, and I had no idea what I could do. Before my daughter was born I had worked as an executive secretary for an American company in Basle, but I had no desire to return to such a highly stressful job which would take too much of my time away from my children. A friend of mine, whose three children also went to the Waldorf School, advised me to try to start my own business. She suggested, 'Why don't you start a cleaning company, honestly committed to using only environmentally friendly products. There is no such service available and I'm sure there would be a demand.' This was very much a win-win situation, as my friend had a small factory making ecological cleaning products and detergents.

I became enthused by the idea. Without a moment of hesitation, I knew that I had found my calling and immediately got to work searching for information as to how to go about it.

Wanting to be a professional cleaning woman was not the easiest thing to do. I had hardly any cleaning experience at all. On our farm in South Africa we had servants. The men worked on the land and their wives did the cleaning and washing for a bag of flour and sugar and a few old pieces of old clothing. The men built a bungalow for their families and were able to use a piece of land to cultivate their own vegetables. If the farmer could afford it, they would receive a few chickens and perhaps a goat to milk.

Starting a cleaning company made me feel like an explorer on a quest. In the very beginning, I was not only the 'boss', I was bookkeeper, secretary, the only employee as well as apprentice. I had so much to learn, not only about starting a business, but also about the right equipment and cleaning agents to be used. To clean a gym hall you would need quite a different kind of broom than what you would use in your kitchen. Then there was the question of employees, benefits and insurance; I had no idea how to tender for a job, not even what prices I could charge. After six months of extensive research and preparation I was offered my first regular contract in March 1988 – it was a Waldorf School.

It was not quite as easy as I had imagined it all to be. At the time, cleaning was not my vocation, and nor did I have a natural talent for it. Contrary to what many people imagine I discovered it was a highly specialised profession, and I also had a lot to learn about people. In addition, it was very important to learn how to conserve my strength, how to protect myself from physical injury as well as from the effects of the atmosphere in the rooms I cleaned. Most of all, I had to learn how to respect the space of other people, how to work in that space and to enter it in a non-judgmental way.

When you clean professionally, you enter a whole new world. What I found hardest to cope with was the indifference I met, the lack of commitment and sometimes even respect. People addressed me in a very familiar way and sometimes men tried to take liberties they would not dream of in another setting. Cleaning can also be a very lonely activity. We cleaning people are often by ourselves when we do our job. Many mothers experience the same kind of loneliness when they are busy with their daily household chores.

During the first years of business, I worked mainly with mothers in a similar situation as mine whose children were more or less the same ages. One of these mothers had to finance her driver's licence, another wanted to buy a piano for the family. Whenever we had a large project, four or five mothers would go out to work, while one stayed at home with all our children. She received the same pay as the mothers who went out cleaning. This was a very special time for all of us. We all had the same attitude to our work and were fired by our ideals. Yet, at some point the piano was bought, the driver's licence obtained, the children started going to school and the need for babysitters became less of a problem. The mothers dropped away, and after about five years, the structure of the company underwent a complete change. I started working mainly with students who had time during the summer holidays and who needed money to finance their studies.

Indifference

About six months after I started my cleaning company, I had a profound identity crisis. Being confronted with the lack of respect was more difficult to handle than I imagined. The constant indifference I encountered was hurtful. Although the clients knew that I was coming to clean, nothing was picked up. I sometimes had the feeling it was done on purpose.

As soon as one cleans for a living, people tend to think that one either cannot do anything else, or that one is in desperate need of money. At this time I often had the impression that people did not quite know how to act with me. Outside on the parking lot they would greet me, and even stay for a chat, yet once I was inside the school building wearing my cleaner's coat and pushing my cleaning cart, they reacted quite differently. The same people seemed to be ill at ease. I was not embarrassed, yet some people did not even bother to greet me. All the other people in the hallway would be greeted, yet the people cleaning were not worthy of a greeting. Sometimes I had the feeling that we were invisible. I even wondered if we were avoided because we reminded people that we were doing something that had very much to do with each and every one of them.

Please do not get me wrong. I have nothing against being employed to clean or that other people wish to employ a cleaner. On the contrary, I find it quite important that people who do not like to clean, or are too busy to do it, should employ others to do so. Without the opportunity to clean for others, I would never have gained the experience I have today. Yet I do find it interesting that the very people who employ us to clean for them often seem to have more reservations about it than we who do the job.

A lack of commitment

A lady once asked me if I would clean her house on a weekly basis. Her husband travelled a lot and besides their three children, they also had a lot of animals living in the house. She hoped that, as a professional person, I would be able to handle this job, as the many other people she had employed before me never seemed to last longer than a month. I took a good look at the house and we agreed that I would clean every Wednesday from 2 till 6 pm. I was very surprised to find the house in total chaos when I arrived for the first time. The lady was out, dirty dishes from at least three days were standing around and the floor was covered with everything imaginable. I could not believe my eyes. In almost all the rooms there were dirty dishes, sometimes even with leftovers. I started by picking up everything that was lying on the floor and by the time I finished all the dishes, two hours had passed. The lady arrived about five minutes before I was to leave and was most vexed that I had not been able to clean the whole house as agreed.

I did point out that the agreement clearly stated cleaning, not picking up or washing dishes. She tried to argue, but I was quite adamant. When I turned up the next week to find the house in exactly the same state as before, I left the key in the mailbox and simply went home.

The lack of commitment with regard to the environment is something I find quite alarming and disturbing. Surely most adults today are aware of the impact of pollution, yet many do very little or nothing at all to improve matters. It is quite amazing to see the kind of very aggressive cleaning and personal hygiene products there are in many homes and institutions I visit. One of the most common excuses is that eco friendly products are either too expensive or not efficient enough. This is either ignorance or quite simply not wanting to try something new. After cleaning professionally for over twenty years, I very rarely resort to a non-ecological product.

There was a time when I cleaned in the early hours of the morning while my family was at home sleeping. This is something that countless people do every day of their lives. To me it was new and I only did it because at that time I could not afford any childcare. As soon as I put the children to bed, I would also go to sleep. Then at about midnight I would get up and go to clean the school until about five in the morning, allowing me to get back before my children and husband woke up.

This school was slightly isolated and at first I would go through the whole school to make sure all windows were closed and that there was no one hiding somewhere. I found that during this time my sense of hearing became much more acute. Everything was so quiet and sometimes I had the experience, cleaning this big school all by myself in the middle of the night, that I could almost hear the rooms speak to me. I learned to distinguish the quality of a sound. Was it threatening or reassuring? In winter, for instance, when the heating system would come on with a shuddering sound at about four in the morning, I would know that it was just about time to go home.

Three questions

While walking up and down long corridors during these nightly hours of service, I discovered that I had a lot of time to think. I tried to understand the deeper meaning of the work I was doing, as my thoughts searched for something beyond my immediate deeds and actions. I also remembered things I had heard and learned before, but which now took on a completely new meaning.

I found myself asking, is this really what I want to do for years to come? Am I willing to carry on picking up after strangers, cleaning away other people's dirt, and putting up with their indifference as I try to render a service?

Three questions arose while I cleaned:

How am I going to handle this indifference, the lack of respect and commitment of others?

What effect does the state of a room have on people?

What changes am I able to bring about in a room, through my own activity of caring for the space?

Regarding the second question, I experienced rooms as very different and often wondered what effect a specific classroom would have on the children who had to learn there. Does the condition of a bedroom influence the child who sleeps there? What about an office or a therapy room? Every word spoken in a room, every thought, every feeling, every moment of passion, or every smoked cigarette leaves traces in a room. Some of what lives in a room we might wish to conserve; but would other influences be better discarded or transformed?

Pondering the third question, could my work positively influence the room and the activity which would take place in it?

These questions were crucial to me. Through living with these questions, a space was created that, little by little, made it possible for the answers to come.

The most important question, of course, was the first one. The answer to it came in the form of a sentence which I had either heard or read somewhere: if you are not able to do what you love, you should try to learn to love what you do.

A good thought, but much easier said than done. I could hand a student her trolley, show her twenty toilets with the request, 'Please clean all these toilets, and make sure you love what you do.' This is impossible! Changing our attitude towards what we do has to rise from the innermost part of our being. Nobody can tell us how to do it.

A legend I had heard a long time ago helped me discover how I could learn to love cleaning.

In a monastery, there lived a monk who was given all the menial tasks, such as washing the dishes, sweeping and scrubbing the floors, and so on. He did not mind this, and did all his chores lovingly, always reciting little prayers while doing his work. 'Dear God, as I wash this dish, please send one of your angels to wash my heart and make it pure.' Or 'Dear God, as I clean this floor, please send one of your angels to accompany me, that every person who walks on this floor may be touched by your presence.' For every chore, he had a prayer, and he continued working in this way for a great many years. Then, one morning, he woke up enlightened. From then on people came from far and wide to listen to his wisdom.

This story reminded me of an experience I had as a child. On our little farm we had paraffin lamps and if the glass was not cleaned every day, the light of the flame would hardly shine through. This, I thought, is what must have happened to the monk in the legend. With so many angels cleaning and scrubbing at him over so many years, it was inevitable that his wisdom would shine through his whole being. This was when I understood that everything we do also reflects on our inner being.

Another memory that came back to me was that my grandmother came to stay with us on the farm after my grandfather had died in an accident. My mother called my three elder sisters and me and explained that our grandmother was very sad and that she cried a lot. We could comfort her by taking turns to make her bed for her every morning. As we had never made our own beds, my mother took us to grandmother's room and showed us exactly how to make the bed. In those days there were no duvets and we had to take great care to fold the linen sheets and the blankets in just the right way, so that the corners would look perfect and the top sheet was folded back to show the embroidery. Most important of all, she explained, was the pillow. Mother took it to the window and showed us how to shake it vigorously and tap it thoroughly so that all grandmother's pain, her tears and her sadness would fly away with the wind. We then had to place the pillow back and smooth it, gently saying a little prayer for grandmother, that she may be comforted when she laid her head down to rest.

I was almost five years old then and I had forgotten this experience for thirty odd years, only to remember it now, while I lived with the challenge of how to learn to love cleaning. Not only the memory of making the bed came back to me, but also the feeling of absolute devotion with which I did it. As a small child, I considered this a sacred chore and I poured my whole energy into this act of comfort I was to do for my grandmother. And now, as a reminiscing cleaner, I knew with total conviction that if only once I could experience this sense of loving devotion while doing my work, would I really learn to love cleaning.

I started doing things in this way. In the beginning, it was merely an exercise which I did faithfully, trying to be very aware of everything I did. I tried to shake something out of certain objects, wipe away or sweep something out. Working with total awareness and devotion was like an act of survival and it gave me something to hold on to. Through repetition it turned into a necessity, and as I started to discover the deeper meaning of what I was doing. I realised that I actually began to draw strength from my work. This newly found strength filled me with profound gratitude, and with this feeling of gratitude I discovered for the first time in months that I was able to experience joy. The longer I did my work with this attitude, the more strongly I was able to feel part of what I was doing. But the most important thing of all was that it enriched my being, my spirit, and this could never be taken away.

Many months later, as I was cleaning my daughter's kindergarten as a dutiful Waldorf parent, I discovered those tiny little toilet bowls. Since then I have found them in many day care centres, but at that time, I had never seen anything like that before. There was something profoundly moving about those little toilet bowls. Being very tall, I thought the only way to clean them in a worthy manner would be to kneel down in front of them. It was then that the image of my little daughter appeared before me. It seemed such a short time ago that I still used to change her nappy and now her little bottom would sit right here on this tiny toilet bowl. At that moment, I experienced this feeling of total devotion. It washed over me like a powerful wave and for the first time I became aware of the fact that we almost always clean for other people.

I understood that cleaning is an eminently social activity. Of course we also clean for ourselves, but even when we live alone, we make a greater effort to clean our homes really well when we are expecting visitors.

This experience also made it clear that cleaning always takes place on different levels. First I take away something physical, removing layers of old dirt. At the same time I strive to clean something within myself, and finally I also wish to leave a gift behind for the people who use the space I have cared for. Today, more than twenty years later and enriched through countless experiences, I can say in all honesty that I still love cleaning.

Only we can decide to what extent we take this occupation seriously. For me, caring for a space is primal. Every living organism thrives when it is cared for, be it a child, a plant, an building serving a community like the Goetheanum, a school or our home – and even, most importantly, our relationships.

Cleaning and caring

After a certain time, I discovered that there is a great difference between cleaning and caring. When we clean, we remove dirt, and the result of cleaning sometimes does not even last five minutes. You have barely cleaned the hallway when someone walks over it leaving footmarks everywhere. As soon as the kitchen floor shines, a small child comes in to proudly present us with a precious treasure found in the sandpit. For this very reason, many people consider cleaning a frustrating and unrewarding activity, a troublesome necessity.

Yet if we try to do this task with our full awareness and devotion, and consciously try to penetrate each little corner with our fingertips, then cleaning takes on a nurturing aspect and becomes caring. While caring for a room, we don't only come into contact with the physical world. The whole atmosphere changes, as if the room is filled with light. Children especially react strongly to this transformation, and they also seem to perceive the change directly. We once gave a big house a very thorough spring clean. Returning from school, the ten-year-old boy immediately wanted to know whether the walls had been painted, as the house seemed so bright and shiny.

When we have taken special care of a room, the little bit of fresh dirt which is brought in is barely disturbing; one can easily live with it. The aura is totally different from areas where layers of dirt and grime have built up. The wonderful thing about caring for a space is that the result of caring lasts considerably longer than 'just' removing dirt.

An elderly lady heard about my way of working and asked me to come in and spring clean her house. Somebody had told her that a house remains cleaner longer when entrusted to my care. I took great care to clean her home as well and thoroughly as possible. Ten days later she called me and said, 'So it is true after all. You know, Linda, I have someone who comes in and helps me with the cleaning every week, but after only three days, I can see dust building up everywhere. I have been checking carefully every day, and today I saw the dust for the first time.'

The amazing thing was that as soon as I learned to love cleaning, the clients also noticed a difference. An architect, whom I had only seen on the day I had signed the contract, suddenly appeared one evening while I was cleaning to ask how I was, and to thank me for the valuable work I was doing.

My new 'reputation' also had some negative effects. The company was now growing steadily and I had to delegate some of my work to new colleagues. I received complaints because some clients claimed that it was no longer as clean as before. Only in one case was this true, because I do not clean 'cleaner' than other people. I believe that probably subconsciously they had noticed that the way I was doing my work had resulted in a different atmosphere in their rooms.

When we care for a space, we do not simply remove dirt, we also create space for something new. What becomes 'new'? Who is going to fill this space? This is quite an important question. I tried to be very open-minded, as far as this was concerned. The answer to these questions came a few years later. But as soon as I had learned to do my work with love and surrender, I also learned to enter a space in a non-judgmental way. Every room I entered became my task and the worse a room looked, the more interesting this task became. I never experienced disgust, not even for the worst possible toilets. I never thought, 'Goodness, what a bunch of pigs.' I simply accepted that this was now the task at hand.

The Goetheanum

In 1992 I was asked if I would take over the responsibility of cleaning the Goetheanum in Dornach, near Basle. The Goetheanum is a cultural centre, seat of the international anthroposophical movement and the home of the School of Spiritual Science and the General Anthroposophical Society. To me, this was not only a great honour; it was the culmination of my task.

My company had already taken over the cleaning of all the sanitary areas in the Goetheanum since 1989 and I chose to step in for my colleague when she was either ill or on holiday. There were a total of sixty-four toilet bowls and it is here that I had learned to always kneel down in front of a toilet in order to clean it. Bending down, straightening up, and moving backwards in a semi circle made me feel quite dizzy. I was not trained then as I am today and I very soon noticed how very strenuous all this bending down was for my back. So I knelt down in front of the toilet to clean it properly and to make sure I could reach every part of it: the very bottom of the bowl, under the edges, the hinges, right to where it was attached to the floor or the wall. This position made a whole world of difference. I perceived the toilet in a totally different way, not only as far as the senses are concerned. I had to adapt my gestures and even touch it in a different way. Once the job was finished I tried to consciously stand upright. All this was a new experience. I developed a strong awareness of my own uprightness and at the same time I could sense how the atmosphere in the room changed. I repeated this exercise often to make sure I was not imagining things. Yet every time on being upright I experienced this change which took place in the space.

I shared this experience with a friend who had studied to become a social therapist and had the privilege of learning from Karl König in a Camphill community. She was able to explain to me that from an esoteric point of view, every act that is consciously done has an effect on the atmosphere, even to the extent where people can feel it and be influenced by it. I believe that this effect can be compared to therapeutic work. A patient who is too weak to move can experience the effect of certain exercises just by observing the therapist executing them.

About five years after I had started my company, while covering for my colleague at the Goetheanum, I had an experience which was to have a strong influence on my life. In a dream, Aïvanhov, the Bulgarian philosopher and mystic mentioned earlier, who had by now passed away, came to me and said, 'The time has come to understand the importance of the work you do.' He took me with him, opened a heavy wooden door and showed me a room I had never seen before. It had a very high ceiling, heavy furniture and impressive paintings on coloured walls. We stood on the threshold and his gaze moved over the entire room. He seemed to greet the room and then started dusting an area with harmonious, flowing, yet very precise gestures. Objects were very lovingly picked up and wiped clean with a soft cloth.

'When you clean,' he said, 'you do not merely remove dirt; you not only "recreate" the objects you touch, you also consciously create space for something new. There are invisible beings that are connected to every room, every object, every human being and even the activities which are to take place in this space. There are helping beings and there are hindering beings. Removing dust and dirt results in a void, and you cannot know what this void, this newly created space, needs. But you can put it at the disposal of the helping spiritual beings that are linked to the place you are cleaning. They know exactly what the people, the space or the activities need, that something new and positive may come about. Do not to merely offer the space to the invisible beings, but take care to offer it only to those beings that are beneficial to the circumstances.'

Before leaving the room, he paused again for a short moment on the threshold, to make sure that all was well and in its proper position, just as we had found it.

The following morning, while I was still cleaning the toilets, the person responsible for the cleaning of the Goetheanum at the time came to me and asked me whether I could take on another task once the toilets were done, as quite a few of the students in the cleaning team were absent. Imagine my surprise when he showed me the room to be cleaned – it was the very same room in which I had received my lesson on caring and creating space the night before.

Since then I never enter a room with the intention of changing anything. This conscious way of taking care of the spaces in which people work, learn or sleep requires attention and sensitivity. There is no sense in trying to force my own ideas onto a space. Through active surrender I learned that it is possible to transform what is found. Rather than trying to change something, I try to be reserved, because I do not know what the space requires. Does a classroom need something harmonious, soft and tender, or does it actually need a 'firm' hand, structure? I trust that the supportive beings linked to the room or activity will know what the needs are. It is sufficient to put the space I created at the disposal of these helpful beings. Thus I have learned to work with the attitude of 'Thy will be done.'

Living on an island?

I sincerely believe that one can identify with the activity of cleaning in a much more profound way than is generally believed. Being a mother and a homemaker does not always receive the recognition it deserves. Too often I hear remarks such as, 'how lovely it must be to be at home all the time and not having to work.' I can very well understand any woman who says, 'I have studied and I have the right to practice my profession; I have as much right to a career as my husband.'

On my way home from a conference, I started talking to a woman opposite me on the train. She had a degree in theology, and was also on her way home after having lectured at a conference on religious education for preschool children. She happened to be the third female theologian that I had met within a month and I found it quite remarkable that all three of them were feminists of conviction.

I spoke about my work, and mentioned that I found it regrettable that the state was quite willing to pour millions into day care centres for very young children, rather than investing the money in prolonged maternity leave to support those who wanted to be full-time mothers. The vehemence of her reaction and her question astounded me: 'Do you live on an island?'

She claimed that my ideas had nothing at all to do with the reality of today and that it was foolish to hanker after conditions which have long since become obsolete. She claimed that women did not want to stay at home anymore; they have earned their right to have a profession and a career. According to her, studies proved that children that grow up in day care centres (especially those who stay all day) not only developed better social skills, but were more intelligent and less inclined to be racist. She claimed that young women who had grown up in this way were totally convinced that this was the right way to do it, and that they would definitely do the same with their children.

Her outburst left me feeling a little shaken. Had I really lost touch with reality? But then why did I receive so many invitations to talk about my work, to talk about a subject that is so very closely related to the work in the home? And why did so many young mothers come? I also had a profession and I also worked away from home while my children were still quite young. I had chosen to be self-employed so that I could remain independent, and schedule my time according to the needs of my children.

This very important service of cleaning was a rich source of learning for me on different levels during these past twenty years. Moreover, it is in cleaning and caring that I have found my personal spiritual path. Almost every day I was able to experience that while we are rarely up to our tasks, we actually grow with them.

If more people could discover and recognise the profound meaning and social importance of homemaking, women who work at home without pursuing a career would receive more recognition. This could lead them to find greater contentment and a sense of fulfilment in their daily chores.

During lectures and workshops on cleaning, I try to communicate what I do and experience in this work. Many people seem to recognise themselves in my little stories, thus finding it easier to understand and express their own experiences. It often offers them the opportunity to structure their everyday life in a new way and even introduces them to totally new possibilities.

For me it is important to do my task in a Christian way, the way I was brought up. Other people may do it in the same way, but connecting themselves to higher spiritual beings that they have chosen on their paths. What is the deeper meaning of our acts? Do we simply do a job or to we strive to work in a salutary way? When we clean, create order, care for our surroundings, what does this mean to the spiritual world?

Every repetitive action can either become routine which has a dulling effect, or when done with love and awareness can become a spiritual path. If I strive to joyfully transform chaos into order, to make what is old and dirty fresh and beautiful, if I try to prevent degeneration and decay, and try to imbue the things that surround me with fresh life, surely this is no less worthy than when a doctor or therapist helps a human being to regain health?

Cleaning is such an important part of our domestic lives, yet many people tell me, 'When I am at work, I do not have any problems with getting things done: I can work for hours with total concentration. But at home everything seems so much more difficult, and then it does not seem to be so important anymore.' Yet our home is and remains the place where we at least should be able to rest and regenerate. Here we can practice 'charity begins at home'. The qualities we develop through the effort of working in our home with love and devotion, will have the stamp of credence.

A further social aspect of caring is the atmosphere that it creates. We are better able to recover from illness in a pleasant atmosphere. My mother claimed that a sick child healed faster in a fresh bed and a clean room. My neighbour once told me that she could not understand why, every time her son was ill, he insisted on sleeping in the living room on the sofa. Knowing her house, it was quite clear to me. He was responsible for the upkeep of his room and it was usually quite chaotic, whereas the living room was clean and orderly.

Cleaning and caring are an essential service to the people around us, in the same way as conscious, environmentally friendly cleaning is essential to nature.

Our home not only gives us shelter and protects us from the elements; in our home, we are who we are. The home offers us this space where we can be nourished and strengthened in soul and spirit. The fundamental importance of the home is that this is where a new society is formed, for it is in our home that our children grow up to build a new generation. It is here that we should offer them the opportunity not only to grow up physically, but to learn to think in a healthy way. Here they can develop as healthy, socially capable beings well able to fulfil their future tasks. There can be no greater deed than to offer a healthy home for the future of humanity, and if we do not take time to do this, we may spend a lot of time regretting it. Through the nurturing aspect of cleaning with care, a good social foundation can be built. We no longer have to exhaust ourselves fighting dirt and disorder, but can learn to transform our handling of it and create space for something new and positive to manifest.

What does it mean to be socially capable? How do we build a social foundation? What are the responsibilities we need to take on when we decide to start a family, and bring children into this world?

Today it is certainly not considered glamorous to be 'just' a mother, a homemaker. We are not in the limelight cleaning toilets or changing diapers. In our homes we are confronted with ourselves and with life. In this span between the daily necessities of life and our striving for harmony, order and beauty, we discover caring. Both parenting and caring have to do with creating an atmosphere, transforming inner and outer spaces.

Nurturing care is an alchemical principle. It is a form of magic. But don't starting looking for magical powers in complicated formulas and rituals. The secret of magic lies in our attitude. Once we have discovered the right attitude, we possess the sacred word that enables us not only to communicate with human beings, but also with animals, plants, and inanimate objects. Each person has to discover this attitude for themselves. It is also important to cultivate respect towards everything that exists.

Without doubt, striving for perfection and self-realisation is very important. But is it only possible away from home? Does it not make sense to try to develop and educate ourselves through everything we do? During a conference at the Goetheanum on the importance of homemaking as a profession, Manfred Schmidt-Brabant referred to the homemaker as a priest. Behind me I heard a young mother muttering furiously, 'I have no ambition to be a priest, I simply want to be a good wife and mother. And that is hard enough as it is!'

Yet being a priest is merely a question of attitude. The princess distinguishes herself from the maid by the attitude with which she accomplishes her task. It is this striving to grow and live up to our tasks that makes the difference. Once our tasks have become a matter of the heart, of a higher ideal, we will receive the gift of perseverance.

In his book, Manfred Schmidt-Brabant mentions that in earlier times initiation took place in initiation centres, the old mystery centres. But today initiation takes place in everyday life. He was convinced that the new mysteries must take place in our homes, in our social institutions, and wherever we do our work out of spiritual understanding. A new society can only blossom fully if human beings in the midst of life learn to transform and recast their lives. Nowhere are we as intimately immersed in everyday life as in the household.

What we do for the spiritual world becomes an investment that no one can ever take away. Here we are all equal and all have the same opportunities.

2. Cleaning as a Cultural Impulse

Cleaning has much less to do with hygiene than with a deep cultural heritage. In most of the western world we do spring cleaning and some also still do a thorough house cleaning before or during Advent. Spring cleaning is still a tradition in Germany, the Netherlands as well as in Russia among Orthodox Christians. Generally it is done after the Carnival festivities at the beginning of Lent: fasting for the body and spring cleaning for the house. Like so many other traditions, it has become commercialised, with lots of new tools and cleaning products appearing in the stores in February.

In America, New Zealand, Britain, and in many other cultures spring cleaning was traditionally done before Easter. The older generation was a firm believer in a thorough spring cleaning. About a week before Easter, the process was started. Windows were washed, curtains and light fixtures were taken down, cleaned and re-hung, rugs beaten clean, floors waxed, furniture polished ... the list went on as each corner and crevice of the house received the homemaker's relentless attention. By the time Easter Sunday came, every room of the house sparkled.

An American friend who followed this tradition while her children were small, confessed that the smells of lemon polish, babka baking, hyacinths and bouquets of daffodils on the table, still filled her with certain nostalgia and the need to take out her cleaning utensils.

Cleaning as a tradition dates back thousands of years with some records relating to homemaking in ancient Persia, Egypt and China. Another ancient cleaning tradition is the Jewish practice of thoroughly cleansing the home in anticipation of the Passover. In Buddhism the tradition of mindfulness with regard to cleaning is as old as Buddhism itself, and is still practised today.

Early civilisations

Every day we all perform countless basic gestures which strengthen and reinforce the very foundation of an immensely complex system, a system of order and classification, which ensures that everything has its own designated place within a larger order. Although it might not seem to be of any importance at all, it constitutes the very foundation of civilisation. One gesture follows the other and very few people stop to consider why they do them. We do not talk about them because they are so trivial, commonplace, yet the smallest domestic actions we do every day are essential for our existence.

Civilisation is based on these elementary and most original gestures. Rudolf Steiner observes,

> Only now is karma beginning. Human karma only became possible when human beings began to employ their hands for work. It was an important step in human evolution when the human being changed from a horizontal into a vertical being, and liberated the hands.[1]

At first people created places to protect them from danger and where they could sleep peacefully. As they also shaped and created tools and objects in these places their activity brought about the development of the first rudimentary systems for thinking and classification. Hand and brain connected to determine where things were to be placed. This did not happen in a static and rigid way. André Leroi-Gourhan points out that the transition from purely protective constructions to real huts, which had to be maintained and cared for, coincides with the advent of basic rhythms in life which brought time and space into awareness. The activities which took place around the home were the origin of socialising rhythms.[2] Human beings developed a coordinated way of using the body and objects necessary to maintain it. Leroi states that it would not be exaggerated to claim that order and cleanliness around the home were the cradle of civilisation.

The Neanderthal lived amid his gnawed bones, which he occasionally, if need be, pushed outside a bit. About 30000 years before our time, a revolutionary step was taken when rubbish was stored outside

the home. To those who consider household gestures to be uninter-
esting and insignificant, the suggestion that the prehistoric invention
of the rubbish bin was a decisive evolutionary step for humanity may
seem far-fetched. And yet this gesture caused a notable extension of
a classification system which is linked to the refinement and differen-
tiation of thinking. In the different stages of history, Leroi, discovered
a principle of socialisation which would strive to create an order in
the surrounding universe, starting from a central point. The point
of departure of this conquest for order was the house, its cleanliness
and the order of the things within. Around this central core, larger
circles were formed: farmlands, industries, a transport system, the
transmission of images, the accumulation of data, and so on, yet the
original gestures always remained. Amazingly, intellectually, we still
copy our ancestors when we carry our rubbish outside. On the tip
of the pyramid we have the rational human being, blazing with efficiency and intelligence. Yet all this light seems to make us blind to
the fact that the tip is very small and that pure rationality is only an
infinitesimal part compared to the deeper layers of thinking. Working
in the home requires a lot of plain common sense and enables us to
continually create something new from what is old, even recreate an
object though attentive care.[3]

Order is a differentiated state created out of an undifferentiated state
of chaos. Creating order is a profoundly creative act and can be put on
the same level as artistic creativity; perhaps it may even be considered
as the primal artistic gesture. We intervene by creating order when
we want to shape or structure something according to our own ideas.
Often we are not even aware that we cannot exist without an ordered
system whose the foundation we rebuild every morning, in the way we
handle the things which surround us in the familiar surroundings of our
own home. We simply try to live as uncomplicated a life as possible,
being carried by the flow of these simple, often unconscious gestures.

Before we can start cleaning, we have to pick up; and in order to do
this efficiently, we need a system. The first thing most people do in the
morning is wash their face and hands: so the day actually starts with
cleaning. It is also one of the first things we teach our children. This is
followed by breakfast, and then, clearing the table, washing the dishes,
brushing teeth: once again, cleaning.

This pattern repeats itself throughout the day. And even if we start our day with meditation, we start by creating inner calm, by bringing our thoughts into order. Almost every deed, every chore presupposes some form of ordering or cleaning. At first I was quite unaware of this, but once I learned to consciously observe my gestures while cleaning, it soon became clear to what extent daily life needs order and cleaning as a foundation. Cleaning is a fundamental cultural experience. This activity is threatening to disappear, not only for many children, but for a large part of society.

If we regain an understanding of the attitude towards it, we may rediscover the essential cultural character of cleaning and caring. Through these daily activities, we elevate nature to culture and we can discover that this is an area where human care unconditionally connects itself with matter.

Purity in Islam

One of the best known traditions of spiritual and physical purification of the Muslim culture is the Turkish bath, the hamam. It can be described as a place for cleansing, purification and body treatments. It is not only an ordinary bath, it is also a centre for healing, social and cultural activities. The benefits of hamam have been known for thousands of years.

Islam places great emphasis on cleanliness in both its physical and spiritual aspects. The hadith, the religious tradition states, 'purification is half of faith.' On the physical side, Islam requires Muslims to clean their body, their clothes, their house and the whole community: God will reward them for doing so.

While people generally consider cleanliness a desirable attribute, Islam insists on it, making it an indispensable fundamental of the faith. A Muslim is required to be pure morally and spiritually as well as physically. Whether or not a woman is employed outside the home, her daily activities focus first and foremost on the material, moral and spiritual needs of the family members. A Muslim woman has the power to make her home a heaven or a hell, according to her own piety and actions. The most important aspect of good hygiene is cleanliness. In Islamic belief the condition of the body affects the mind, physical cleanliness is essential for spiritual well-being.

Muslim homes are very clean and considered almost sacred. Before entering a Muslim home the shoes worn on the street are removed. When going to the toilet special shoes that never enter any other part of the home are used. Bathing or washing items must not be done in stagnant water. Everything washed in a bowl is rinsed afterwards under a running tap. (For this reason you will not generally find plugs for sinks.)

Other traditions

Other societies believe that the house should not be cleaned nor the trash thrown away after sundown. An Orthodox Jewish friend explained the importance of not leaving dead flies in the house after the sun went down.

In certain cultures it is even important to consider the days on which certain activities should be done. For instance, Sunday is neither good for bathing nor for washing clothes, on Mondays one should neither buy nor wear new clothes, and while Tuesday is not particularly good to visit families, Wednesday is considered a good day to visit the doctor.

In Nepal, a housewife's first duty in the morning is to sweep the house from the lowest story up, not from the upper stories downwards, because that is done only on the day that a death has occurred in the house. Next she cleans her water pots and pitchers and fetches water in them. Water must be brought fresh every morning because what is kept overnight is unfit for drinking and cooking rice. She uses ash to clean the brassware, not soap, because it is considered impure. Every now and then, especially when there is a ceremony or feast, the mud floor all over the house is washed with a mixture of cow dung and red earth.

For the Mayans at the time of Columbus, spring started with the first month of the New Year, the month of Pop, a time of renewal in both the figurative and the literal sense. Dishes, woven mats and clothes of the past year were destroyed, and new pots, woven mats and clothes were made.

Japanese misogi

A Japanese student first told me about a tradition called misogi. It is a spiritual practice of ritual purification as preparation for meditation. She explained that cleaning is one of the most important traditions of Japanese culture. Practising misogi by cleaning is a way to create a good and healthy environment. Cleaning by hand with a damp cloth is considered an opportunity for meditation.

Her explanations helped me to understand why so many leading water researchers, like Masaru Emoto, come from Japan. Effective micro organisms and electrolysed water systems also come from Japan. Bacteria and insects thrive during the hot and humid Japanese summer and survive well in the cold and dry winter. As the main purpose of cleaning is to create a healthy environment, it changes the general attitude Japanese have towards cleaning.

Japanese culture is rooted in dualism, like yes/no, good/bad, positive/negative, etc. This is found in the Japanese language. Not good means bad. Not bad means good. Dualism can also be found in the approach to hygiene. People think they can create a good environment by getting rid of bad things, using the logic of not bad means good. However, while it is important to get rid of bad things, it is not enough, and has to actively create a good environment.

Water ions in the air promote good health. So the basic way of creating a healthy environment is to create more water ions. Humidity between 50 and 70 percent is best for forming water ions. If the air is too dry, there are less water ions, and if the air is too humid, the walls are covered with condensation leaving fewer surfaces with air contact, resulting in fewer ions.

Building materials used inside the house, such as wood and plaster, support the regulation of humidity. When wood or plaster release humidity into the air, it also creates water ions, thus supporting health. Synthetic surfaces are avoided as the chemical fumes are bad for health, whereas metal is considered neutral. Wind also plays an important part in ionisation; through breaking down the water particles and creating ions, it brings relief when humidity is too high.

Another important factor is cleaning by hand with a damp, not too wet, cloth. The friction of a damp cloth on any surface creates ions. It is also important to wipe the surface with enough force to break down the water molecules. According to this Japanese student, the normal European way of using a wet cloth on a long stick to clean the floor is useless because the cloth is too wet and there is not enough friction. People then rely on unhealthy chemical products to get rid of dirt, whereas it is best to use only water, wiping vigorously with one's hands. Using both hands to get rid of surplus water in the cloth is the traditional Japanese way.

She told me that sadly, this part of Japanese culture is getting lost. As many Japanese women have to work and often have no help in the home, they use more chemicals to make their jobs easier.

Greek and Russian customs

In Greece, Clean Monday, also known as Koulouma, was at the culmination of the carnival period, at the beginning of the Lent season (the forty days before Easter). Clean Monday, also called Pure Monday, Lent Monday, Ash Monday, stands for spiritual and physical purification. Some say the word clean was added to that day because housewives had to clean their houses and utensils all day long after Carnival was finally over. Today, for most Greeks, celebrating Clean Monday means going to the hills or sea to enjoy a fasting picnic and fly kites.

A special tradition takes place in Russian parks just before spring starts. You may see Russian ladies of all ages laying their rugs on the snow and beating them with sticks or tennis rackets. Then they flip them over and repeat the beating process. At the end of the day, there are lots of black patches of snow all over the park. It is considered the best and virtually only way to clean the rugs that are scattered all over the house, on the floor and on the walls.

In earlier times, the upper class families in Russia employed migrant workers to help with the spring cleaning, as it is still done during the harvesting season. There was even a guild of floor polishers, as described by Margarita Woloschin (1882–1973).

> No parquet floors can now shine as they did, for the guild
> of floor polishers, the Polotjory, has vanished from the

world. Every week five or six men appeared in our house, barefoot, in wide black velvet pants and red shirts that reached to the knees and hung loose from a belt at the hips. Everything had to make way for them, the carpets were rolled up, furniture was moved against the wall. Lessons were interrupted when this crowd appeared. Each one tied a sandal onto the right foot, which had waxed brushes underneath; and then they moved in a row through the room, hands crossed behind their backs, with the right foot in front making an arc from right to left, from left to right, while pushing themselves forward with the left foot. Strands of hair hung down into their faces and swung back and forth in time with their movements. From time to time one of them remained standing, and busily rubbed with his foot forwards and backwards. All this took place with elemental force and speed, and in this way they danced through hall after hall, room after room. And when they departed from the house, leaving behind an odour of sweat mixed with the smell of wax and turpentine, our floors shone magnificently.[4]

The origin of spring cleaning

There is some disagreement as to the origin of spring cleaning as we know it. Some sources say it originated in Nowruz, meaning 'New Day' that was the traditional Persian new year. This begins exactly at the astronomical spring equinox. Others claim its origin is in the ancient Jewish practice of thoroughly cleansing the home in anticipation of the Passover festival that commemorates the liberation by God of the Jewish people from slavery in Egypt.

The Passover

During the seven-day observance of the Passover there are strict prohibitions against eating or drinking anything which may have been leavened with yeast. Jews must not only refrain from eating leavened food-stuffs (chametz in Hebrew), they must remove even small remnants of chametz from their homes for the length of the holiday. Therefore, observant Jews conducted a thorough spring cleaning of the house.

The big spring cleaning in Jewish tradition requires chametz to be actually searched out and removed or burnt; it is not enough to simply write the chametz off as 'dust'. Not one crumb of chametz should remain in the house. All kitchen surfaces are cleaned thoroughly. The refrigerator and freezer must be defrosted and cleaned out thoroughly. If separate Passover utensils are not used, the usual ones need to be immersed in boiling water. Doorknobs, light switches and upholstery have to be cleaned very well and the cushions from the couch have to removed, checked and vacuumed. Finally, when everything else in the house has been prepared for Passover, the floors are thoroughly washed. After all the cleaning the broom and the garbage can are cleaned as well, and the vacuum cleaner bag is thrown out.

On the eve of the holiday there is the traditional hunt for chametz crumbs by candlelight (called bedikat chametz). During the Passover holiday they can only eat food that is kosher for Passover, that is food that contains no chametz.

Persian New Year traditions

Most New Year traditions include cleaning, and in many oriental countries the New Year coincides with spring. In Iran (Persia), before the actual Nowruz family gatherings and celebrations, there is an extensive top to bottom, thorough spring cleaning, Khouneh Tekouni, literally meaning 'shaking the house'. This ritual is for everyone and every household, whether they live in a simple room with minimal furnishings or in a palatial mansion filled with luxurious items. This once-a-year cleaning ritual is more than the typical routine of vacuuming, mopping and dusting. In the homes of many Iranians, the process of spring cleaning starts weeks before the celebration, so by the time Nowruz arrives, the house would be sparkling clean, organised and neat, the children dressed in their new spring clothes. The Haft-Seen, the traditional table setting for Nowruz, has seven symbolic items. In ancient times each item corresponded to one of the seven creations and the seven holy immortals protecting them. All seven items start with the Persian letter seen. Zoroastrians today do not have the seven seens but they have the ritual of growing seven seeds as a reminder that this is the seventh feast of creation, while their sprouting into new growth symbolised resurrection and eternal life to come.

The ritual of spring cleaning would start with the lady of the house going through all the closets and chest of drawers one by one. She would take everything out, get rid of the old and worn out clothing, put the winter clothes away and neatly return the 'good' clothing. Then she would clean the rugs, draperies, shades, windows, refrigerator, stove, kitchen cabinets and appliances. Not to mention, the occasional fresh coat of paint for the living room and dining room and the re-upholstery of some of the chairs.

These processes are also a symbolic reminder to take in the spirit of spring and clear the hearts and minds, and to let go of accumulated grudges and hard feelings, and to start the New Year with a new attitude and positive outlook on life. The conscious housemother welcomes the Nowruz celebrations with joy, taking in the fresh new air of the coming New Year, and facing the challenging task of living fully in the moment with every breath.

Persians celebrate the ten days before the New Year with the feasts and bonfires. The celebration culminates on the last Wednesday of the year, called Chaharshanbeh Suri. Bonfires are built on Tuesday night and people leap over the flames. Earlier in the evening, children and adults, wrapped in shrouds, run through the streets, beating on pans and pots with spoons to 'beat out' the unlucky Wednesday. (A similar tradition is also still practised in certain parts of Switzerland, where children use cow bells to ring out the winter.)

China and Vietnam

Between the Laba festival, on the eighth day of the last lunar month, and lunar New Year families throughout China undertake a thorough house cleaning, sweeping out the old in preparation for the New Year. According to Chinese folk beliefs, during the last month of the year, ghosts and deities must choose either to return to heaven or to stay on earth. In order to ensure the timely departure of the ghosts and deities, people had to thoroughly clean both themselves and their dwellings down to every last drawer and cupboard. As New Year's Eve approaches all family affairs must be put in order, to ensure a fresh start in the New Year. The cleaning includes organising the yard as well as scrubbing the doors, windows, and interior of the house. Old decorations and paper cuts from the previous New Year festival are taken down, and new window decorations, New Year's posters, and auspicious decorations are pasted up.

A week before the New Year, Xiao Nian, Preliminary Eve, is also known as the festival of the Kitchen God. This deity oversees the moral character of each household. In one of the most distinctive traditions of spring festival, a paper image of the Kitchen God is burned on Xiao Nian, dispatching the god's spirit to heaven to report on the family's conduct over the past year. The Kitchen God is then welcomed back by pasting a new paper image of him beside the stove. From this vantage point, the Kitchen God will oversee and protect the household for another year.

The Vietnamese New Year, or Tết, is a lunar New Year based on the Chinese and occurring in late January or February. Homes are often cleaned and decorated before New Year's Eve. Children are in charge of sweeping and scrubbing the floor. The kitchen needs to be cleaned seven days before Tết, the 23rd of the last lunar month. Each family offers a farewell ceremony for Ong Tao, the kitchen guardian, to go up to the heavenly palace. His task is to make an annual report to the Jade Emperor, the ruler of heaven, of the family's affairs throughout the year. Usually, the head of the household cleans the dust and ashes (from incense) from the ancestral altars. It is a common belief that cleaning the house will get rid of the bad fortunes associated with the old year. Some people paint their houses and decorate them with festive objects.

For children, this is often the most exciting festival. Parents purchase new clothes and shoes for their children to wear on the first day of the New Year.

New Year's Eve is the moment of seeing the old chief end his ruling term and pass his power to the new chief, for each year is ruled by a different sacred animal. It is also the time for Ong Tao to return after making his report to the Jade Emperor. Each family offers an open-air ceremony to welcome him back into their kitchen. As flower buds and blossoms are the symbols for new beginning every home will be filled with them.

A special ceremony is held on the first day of the New Year before noon. The head of the household ritually offers food and wine, and burns incense to invite the souls of the ancestors to join the celebration with the family.

Japan

Osoji, literally meaning free and clean, is the year-end cleaning of the house in Japan. It includes the whole house, especially the areas that are not cleaned so often. Osoji also takes place in temples and shrines; an interesting cleaning ritual called susuharai, or beating the dust. In Kyoto at the Higashi and Nishi Honganji, the Eastern and Western Temples, it is a huge annual event on December 20. Disciples come from all over Japan, put on long-sleeved clothes, a large face mask and cover their heads with a towel. One group uses long, thin bamboo sticks to beat all the tatami mats in the halls while another group swings huge Japanese fans, two metres across, to blow all the dust away.

India

Deepavali or Diwali, popularly known as the festival of lights, is the most lavish and vibrant of all Hindu festivals. It falls in late October or November. Celebrations and ritual for the festival begins days and weeks in advance. Every household indulges in a list of activities that marks the occasion. Cleaning the homes and offices is a priority. A week before the festivity, the house is cleaned and tidied, and rangoli motives (brightly coloured decorations) are made in living rooms and courtyard floors. The ancient symbols have been passed down from one generation to the next, keeping the art form and tradition alive through the ages. The patterns are typically created with coloured rice, dry flour, coloured sand or even flower petals. They are sacred welcoming areas for the Hindu deities, especially the goddess of wealth Lakshmi, whose blessing is sought.

Celebrations last for five days, each serving a different purpose such as buying new utensils, bursting crackers, wearing new clothes and indulging in ceremonial activities.

Christmas

A German friend told me the great joy they shared as a family during days of cleaning the house as a preparation for Christmas. Her mother explained that space had to be created for new toys and that they would only be brought into very clean rooms. No task was too big for her and her siblings. Together they cleaned every room from the cellar to the attic, rejoicing in the cookies and hot chocolate to be shared after their efforts.

Christmas is very traditional in Sweden and many Swedes believe that the preparation should be at least as joyful as the real thing. This is important because many an ambitious housewife risk being too exhausted to enjoy the actual festivities. General Christmas preparations can be divided into three categories – decorations, gifts, and food and entertaining. And tucked somewhere in there is the thorough cleaning of the house including changing curtains and draperies.

A Czech Christmas is not complete without engaging in a full and extensive house cleaning. Often this cleaning takes up to a week, and only then is time to start the other Christmas preparations.

In Puritan Scotland Christmas was virtually banned from the end of the seventeenth century to the 1950s as a Popish or Catholic feast. Instead Scots celebrated New Year when family and friends gathered at Hogmanay. Traditions before midnight include a thoroughly cleaning the house on December 31, including taking out the ashes from the fire. It was also a practice to clear all debts before 'the bells' at midnight.

In all the cultures where cleaning is part of the preparation for a festival we see the care in creating a space for something new to enter. It was felt that only then the beneficent spirits could enter the space. This reminded me of the dream I had about the importance of creating a space for the helping beings who accompany us when we do our work.

3. Human Beings, Home and Helpers

*Nature is alive and we should meet her with respect. You might
say you don't think that your respect towards nature could make a
change. Then at least do it for yourself. If you are attentive towards
stones, plants, animals, people and even towards the objects that
surround you, you will develop your awareness, enlarge it and your
whole life will be enriched through these experiences, and everything
around you will breathe and become vibrant. As long as you have
not understood this, do not be surprised that you sometimes feel ill at
ease, disorientated, or filled with a feeling of emptiness.*

*Would you like to give your life some meaning? Then consider
that you are connected to all the forces and delightful beings
of nature and that you can communicate with them. In this
uninterrupted communion with so many different beings you will
taste and savour a true life. You may want to know how you could
achieve this. It is through respect and love: there is no other way.
If you respect nature, if you love nature, she will speak to you and
then you too will become part of nature.*

Omraam Mikhaël Aïvanhov (1900–1986)[1]

Wisdom, devoutness and life confidence

Human beings are the culmination of creation. In many creation myths
and traditions man received the task to take care of the earth and its
creatures. In Genesis the caring of the Garden of Eden was entrusted
to man.

Today people seem to have forgotten this duty. Instead of caring and
maintaining the earth and its creatures, our attitude too often is to use

it for our own interest. We need nature in order to survive, for nourishment and shelter. But to a certain extend we have taken this too far. At some point we seem to have lost balance. Species are dying, forests are ailing and we hear of more and more nature catastrophes. Great areas have become wasteland, having lost all fertility and consequently being deserted. Today more and more people are awakening to these perils, and try to remind us of this original task. Nature needs human beings just as human beings needs nature. We must keep the balance of giving and receiving.

Some years ago at the Goetheanum I was collecting all the old paper which is then put into large paper bags, to be compressed and then collected by a recycling company. As I was pouring the paper into one of these large bags, a small brochure slipped out onto the floor. I had a close look at it and saw that it was in English and decided to take it home with me. A little voice immediately told me to at least have a look and see if there was something in the booklet that I could use. I paged through it and found a lecture entitled Anthroposophy in daily life by Rudolf Steiner. I tore out the pages and took them home with me. There I read them, and I've read them many times since. I was convinced that there must be at least some words said about cleaning, but this was not the case. The lecture started with the following words: 'If we really grasp spiritual science it gives us strength and confidence in life. How can we introduce it into our life so that it may help us to advance?' I was expecting practical exercises, but there was no trace of it and not even a word was mentioned about cleaning, but only about how we can learn to develop qualities within ourselves that enable us to contribute to the development of the earth. The lecture finished with the following paragraph:

> We thus strengthen the best forces that we are able to
> develop as human beings for the whole evolution of the
> earth in our astral body, our ether body and our physical
> body through wisdom, devoutness and confidence in life.
> In this way we work upon the planet earth and acquire a
> feeling which shows us that human beings do not lead to
> an isolated existence in the world, but that the forces which
> they unfold within themselves are of value to the whole

world. Every speck of dust bears within it the laws of the universe; similarly every human being builds up or destroys the world by what he does or leaves undone. We may give something for the progress of the world, or deprive it of something, and we may crumble away from it by ignoring it, by failing to acquire confidence in life. These sins of omission contribute to the decay of our planet, whereas what we acquired in wisdom, devoutness and confidence in life, help to build it up. We may thus gradually obtain an idea of what anthroposophy can give us, if it takes hold of the whole human being.[2]

The human being

Many religions and occult teachings describe that there is more to the human being that his physical body. Rudolf Steiner describes four parts.

Firstly, there is the physical body. Its most notable feature is its mortality. The physical body is unable to keep itself alive: left to itself, it would begin to rot, perish and decay into dust, as it does after death.

Secondly, what keeps the physical body alive is an invisible energy, our life body or ether body. It is not made of matter, but consists of life processes, rhythms and processes that take place in time. All living beings are involved in these processes of growing, blossoming and decaying.

But we do not consist only of life processes. We have feelings, desires, dreams – and also the zest to realise these. Our health is influenced by the way we think, form our opinions or accomplish a task at hand. We should not underestimate the influence our thinking, feeling and will can have on our wellbeing. The emotional level of human nature and its influences are centred in the sentient soul or body, also called the astral body.

The fourth part of our being is our individuality, our 'I' or spiritual self. It is our personality, our very identity, and contains all our experiences, our destiny, and all we have learned. The self can relate to or distance itself from the world through the other three parts. In our spiritual self lies the inexhaustible source of life. We stay in touch with it if we live with the questions as to what I, as an individuality, wish do with my life, what are my goals, my ideals?

We are given the opportunity to cultivate our highest goals through doing small tasks and very simple exercises. If our actions are determined not by habit or outer circumstances, but by our innermost self in total freedom, we develop abilities that enable us to permeate our surroundings with a positive quality.

The home as an organism

Build of your imaginings a bower in the wilderness ere you build a house within the city walls.

For even as you have home-comings in your twilight, so has the wanderer in you, the ever distant and alone.

Your house is your larger body.

It grows in the sun and sleeps in the stillness of the night; and it is not dreamless.

Does not your house dream? And dreaming leave the city for grove or hill top?

Khalil Gibran (1883–1931), The Prophet

In 1993, when I was a mere novice at the Goetheanum, I attended the annual conference on the importance of homemaking as a profession, hosted by Manfred Schmidt-Brabant. The idea I heard there, that our home, just like the human being himself, consists of a physical body, a life body, a soul body (astral body) and a spiritual self, was completely new to me.

Our home of course has a physical side, often powerfully obtrusive. This physical body includes all the fittings and furniture. The garden, basement, loft and garage are part of the physical body. The element of earth is a predominant of the physical, which we most strongly experience through its resistance.

If we meet this resistance through conscious work, doing household chores with harmonious movements, penetrating our gestures with awareness, we enter into a rhythmic flow, and begin to experience the ether spaces of our home. This is the life stream of the house, which manifests as order, division, rhythm and habits of the inhabitants – in short, in the way a community is shaped. Just as our body eats, digests, expels, or we breathe in and out, so materials come into our home, are used and are expelled again. Often these processes do not work as well in the home as they do in the body. Much is taken in, but all too often, too little is eliminated: we accumulate too much and often feel burdened that.

We experience the soul or astral body of a house in its atmosphere. Here live the qualities that are brought into it by the individuals who live in it. Traces of their thinking, feelings and activities impregnate it. Especially our artistic activities – the art of cooking or the art of creating order – as well as humour are important. Devotion to small things, reverence and gratitude can enhance the atmosphere of a home.

How do we experience the spirit of a house? Through the relationships between the household members, and also in the way all the aspects of culture live in a home. Is art cultivated in the house? What lives in the social sphere of the family? Do they respect each other? Are ideals and spirituality part of conversations? Is grace said before meals? Is there awareness of the guardian angel who leads everyone through life, or of the deceased who are connected with us?

Every person who manages a household is faced with various daily tasks. But for those who are willing to openly embrace it, much can be discovered anew. There are different levels which we can influence with our care and attention, for everything physical always has a spiritual side. So we remove dirt, not only physically, we also work with our life and soul forces, with our self. Our home, its cleanliness and maintenance are not ends in themselves. In our home we create a common space, space for the development of individuals, communities and the spiritual world.

Anyone who experiences the home as an organism treats it in a different manner. Every living organism thrives through care. If we simply water a plant, it will grow, yet if we cultivate it lovingly, it will thrive. From room to room, from classroom to classroom, we can see the difference between surviving, growing and thriving plants. The same applies to the care we give to animals, to children, and very importantly, to our relationships with other people.

After some years of my work I have sometimes felt such a strong relationship with a building or a room that I could sense its needs.

Through perception and self-education we can learn to see how to work on ourselves and our surroundings in order to take the next step.

Uninhabited buildings decay with astonishing rapidity, like a body without life. An empty house decays faster than an occupied house. Even a car that is driven infrequently runs the risk of seizing up and rusting. Clothes worn regularly, even woollen clothes, are less frequently attacked by moths than those that are stored.

In the main auditorium of the Goetheanum (with nearly a thousand seats), it was important to me that someone cleaned there every day. So the floor was swept daily, even if only a few rows each day. Due to economy measures, it was decided that the hall was only to be cleaned before and after an event. Within a few weeks we had a moth infestation in the woollen upholstering of the seats. (The cost of eliminating the moths and subsequently redoing the floor was far greater than the planned savings.)

If we learn to respect our home, school or place of work as a living organism, worthy of being maintained with dedication, our work takes on a quality of devotion that changes the atmosphere and can make a room lighter. Care is always a conscious act, so it not only influences the immediate present, but contributes much to the future. This is true ecology.

Helping beings

As a child I was never told bedtime stories, and I only discovered fairy tales when I had learned to read. But being a member of a large family with many uncles, aunts, nieces and nephews we used to have big family reunions. After the barbecues stories were told around the fire. These were always based on 'real' experiences and often had something to do with the supernatural. As children we could not get enough of those strange ghosts and goblins, and all the premonitions of events to come.

One story that impressed me very much was about a man who was very mean and it was told that he entered into a pact with the devil because his neighbour always had better harvests than he had. One night, as he was busy with his dark practices, his house and he himself caught fire. He ran across a field towards a dam (reservoir) to save himself. But it was in vain, and the grass never grew again in his footsteps from the house to the dam.

Most families in the country could claim to have at least one person with extrasensory perception. My father was a water dowser, and as we lived in was very dry area his services were in demand. He used to tell us that he had a little monkey sitting on his shoulder who would tell him things, such as when a child was coming, when the birth was due, and even if it was going to be a boy or a girl. Unfortunately he was also able to predict more unpleasant events.

We heard a lot of wonderful stories from the servants who lived on our farm. There were giants against whom you needed to protect your animals skilfully. They also told about the Tokolossie, who would catch naughty children and was a nuisance to married women in the city by trying to climb into their beds.

So as a child I heard of the extraordinary beings, many of them amiable and helpful, though some were very bad and mean.

All cultures, religions, customs, myths and legends refer to a complete host of beings, ranging from those light-filled beings who help, protect and guide us to the most dangerous, darkest evil spirits.

Not only are these beings found in fairy tales and legends, but also in the Bible and in literature like Goethe's Faust or Shakespeare's Midsummer Night's Dream. The sixteenth-century alchemist and physician Paracelsus gives a detailed description of these beings and the world they live in. He wrote of Pygmies, Nymphs, Sylphs and referred to water beings as Undines, air beings as Sylvestres, mountain beings as Gnomi and fire beings as Salamanders and Vulcani. Paracelsus describes the homes of these beings precisely, objectively, yet very poetically.

Human longing for a world in which we call on invisible and miraculous creatures to fight evil is found not only in fairy tales but in advertising (dirt devils), books and films such as Lord of the Rings, Harry Potter, or Avatar. Many people long for a communion with nature and nature spirits and it is not impossible for us to experience them directly, as many people already do. But we have to consciously learn to enter into a new kind of relationship with nature and be open to what is new and unknown. We also have to learn to take responsibility for our actions and to know that there are always consequences to everything we think, feel and do. It is easier to dream of these skills through film images rather than making a conscious effort to take life into our own hands.

Perceiving nature beings

Many books tell of encounters people have had with angels and other nature beings, and there are courses which promise to teach you to communicate with nature and angels. To some people this all sounds strange and unusual, even scary Mostly it is because it so far removed from their everyday experience and sounds like science fiction films. But can we form a clearer idea of these invisible helpers without becoming superstitious or spaced out? Is there more to elemental beings than the brightly coloured garden gnomes?

In his book *Theosophy*, Rudolf Steiner makes a remark about the necessary attitude to have regarding the world of elemental beings, 'The superstition ... lies not in believing these beings are real but in believing these beings appear sense-perceptibly.'[3]

It may help to look at experiences that are familiar to us. We all know the feeling of being observed. Sometimes we even feel the direction where the gaze comes from, and often our feeling is confirmed if we manage to turn around fast enough. Another example is the feeling we get when we enter a hotel room or a holiday home. Sometimes we have a strong feeling of discomfort and even unease. If we take a few moments to reflect on our perception and to try to analyse what it is that we feel, we are carefully approaching the unknown and are making a first attempt to discover what lives around us.

The more we practice this, the better we will be able to perceive the human and natural surroundings. It is not always new things that we experience, but we can learn to understand what we have experienced in a new way. By trying to perceive things in a new light, everything can become new.

Communication

Many people might find it hard to accept that one could make similar experiences with plants or that it could be possible to hear a room actually asking for help. To communicate with spaces is simply part of my work and to me this communication is of utmost importance. After taking care of a room for a certain period of time, one starts entering into a relationship with this room and if this relationship is strong enough, communication takes place. I am not at all clairvoyant, but I am certain that a room can express it needs to me even if for others this might sound somewhat strange.

The hand soap we used at the Goetheanum, was quite popular and visitors often wanted to buy some. To fetch it from the storage room we had to pass through the lady's facilities which had fourteen cubicles. I once entered with a visitor, and immediately noticed that something was wrong. I walked up to a door, opened it and found a messy toilet that had not been flushed. I did what was necessary, and to me everything was fine. The lady, however, asked me, 'How could you possibly know that something was not in order, and how did you know it was that specific toilet because all the doors were closed?' I cannot explain this in rationally, but to me this is but a small example of communication with the beings which accompany me in my work every day.

Recently I had a totally new experience. I had a very difficult decision that had to make concerning my future and was very uncertain and even apprehensive. I had no idea with whom I could speak regarding this matter. I went for a walk in the forest and in the distance I noticed something that looked like a little manikin with a small head and a big round stomach. As I approached I noticed that it was only two daisies: a small one that was slightly higher than the bigger round one. I sat down on the grass beside the flowers and spontaneously said, 'Dear little daisy, I am so worried. Who can I possibly talk to?' To my astonishment I received a very clear answer that seems to rise up from within me: speak to Mr X about it. I was completely dumbfounded, as I would never have considered this specific gentleman, but at the same time I felt very relieved and grateful. Two days later I had an appointment with him, and within ten minutes I had explained my situation and was immediately promised all possible support for the proposed project.

When it comes to experiences like this, it's not important whether the flower actually gave me an answer or not, nor do I wish to convince anybody. What is important is what this experience meant to me personally, and that it strengthened my faith in these helping forces.

Similar situations are often described in fairy tales. Often, in a moment of greatest despair or danger, a little nature being appears as an answer to a cry for help. If the person is then willing to follow the advice or is in turn willing to help, they are often richly rewarded.

It is important that we reflect on our experiences and perceptions, that we pay attention to the smallest changes and try to find out what brought about this change. While doing our household chores, it may happen that all of a sudden everything seems to be easier, that it seems to go faster and that we feel less tired. We might even start singing because we experience a sense of joy. Our children might even suddenly offer to help. I have often noticed that when I fully surrendered to the task at hand, somebody unexpectedly offered their help, as if they want to share in the joy.

Let me tell you about the experience a friend had while cleaning windows. For more than a year I looked after her two little children every Wednesday morning. That particularly morning was a beautiful spring morning and on our way home, every little flower and snail was observed with awe and admiration. Fortunately we were in no hurry, and it did not bother me that the children seem to find great joy in all the smaller and bigger things on their way home. We hardly lived five hundred metres away from each other, yet on this morning the children needed more than half an hour to cover the distance. When we arrived home, their mother opened the door with a beaming smile saying, 'I thought that you were having a good time, so instead of just waiting, I decided to clean the kitchen windows. As you were still not home, I continued with the living room, then the dining room, and now look, I have cleaned all the windows.'

The windows were all sparkling clean, and as a professional, I can assure you that time had been given to her. There is no way she could have cleaned all those windows so well in such a short period of time.

In fairy tales we often read about nature beings who wish to help if people are willing to fulfil certain conditions. For instance, it often happens that the Prince finds a beautiful girl to become his wife who is pious and good. Or the Princess is often saved by a young man who is the youngest of three brothers, or is courageous but simple and open towards nature and her beings.

The four classical elements

The doctrine of the four elements – earth, water, air and fire – being the basis for all life on earth goes back to Empedocles, who lived in Greece in the fifth century BC.

We are in daily contact with these elements, and they play an important role in our life, even in the everyday tasks of cleaning, tidying up, washing our hair, airing a room, lighting a candle or cooking. In observing a burning candle, we experience all four elements simultaneously: the solid wax and wick, the liquid wax, air in the movement of the flame and light and heat of the flame itself. The elements serve us, and we can learn to use them more consciously.

Small children have a natural relationship with the elements. They love water and immediately experience the joy that water gives them. On a swing they happily experience flying through the air with the wind sweeping through their hair. Children play imaginative games with the element of earth in the sandpit for hours on end. And they love fire, every child loves lighting a candle and looking at the meandering smoke when it is put out again.

Children can be greedy and wasteful in their dealings with the elements. A child's behaviour is all about immediate experience. Children do not worry about all the water it takes to make a really nice puddle. This has nothing to do with abuse or wastefulness but rather a joyful experiencing which is more reminiscent of a mutual giving and receiving. As children are closer to the natural elements, so the elements seem closer to children.

How wonderful it would be if we as adults were able to rediscover this intimate experience of the elements that we had as children. The elements are everywhere – around us and in us. They make life possible, but can also wipe it out in natural disasters.

In the area where I grew up, there were often long periods of drought. Sometimes it was so dry that even the chickens died. Already as small children we learned to be very economical with water. Each child received a small tumbler of water to brush our teeth, and once a week on Sundays we had the luxury of a bathtub for two. During the week we just had a shallow dish of water for our daily washing.

A remarkable phenomenon, that I only experienced as a child, was an electrical storm. There was thunder and lightning, yet not a drop of rain. Sometimes the air was so charged that our hair stood on end in all directions, and we had to be very careful not to touch any metal fixtures for fear of getting a shock. But then, what blessed moment when the scent of water finally announced the rains. The animals went completely silly: dogs raced across the fields, the cows jumped around like young calves on the pastures. As soon as the first drops fell, the whole family would stand outside, all crowding around father with his hat on his chest, as we all thanked the Lord.

The storms were sometimes so violent that trees were split by lightning or fields were set alight. Roofs were blown off houses and small streams turned into raging torrents. Thus we experienced the elements in full force. When I came to Europe I had to wait for months for a real thunderstorm, and I have only once experienced the intensity of the African elements during a thunderstorm high in the mountains.

What do we know about the elements?

The earth sustains us and gives us our shape; it is the foundation of our existence. In earlier times people were much more directly connected with their surroundings and felt the earth element right into their bones. Water refreshes us and flows through us, air supplies us with the breath of life and surrounds us, and warmth (fire) keeps us alive, allows us to be active and develop our willpower.

Just as the earth is inhabited by different peoples with different characteristics, from the Arctic through the deserts to the equatorial rain forests, so there are elemental beings with different characteristics, depending on the elements with which they are connected.

Aristotle spoke about the four points in space with his pupil Alexander the Great. According to his teaching there is dryness in the east, humidity in the west, cold in the north and warmth in the south. The earth element manifests between dryness and cold. The solidity of the earth also enables us to walk upright, allowing us to be upright beings. The water element works between humidity and cold, and is experienced in the circling, streaming, fluid processes if the body. Air manifests between humidity and warmth – and can be experienced in breathing and speech. Between warmth and dryness, heat and fire are active. Love and will, human activity can be experienced through warmth (fire).

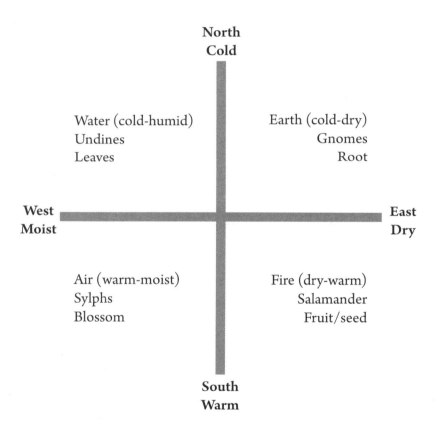

The four classic elements and their related nature spirits and parts of the plant

The four elements are present in all our activities, either separately or combined. We exist as physical beings only because the elements and the angels of the elements make it possible. These angels of the elements are powerful, magnificent beings, and the elements themselves are inhabited by countless living elemental beings. We are never separate from the elemental world, we are just not sufficiently aware of it.

While caring for a space or an object, we are constantly on the threshold of the elemental, spirit world. Becoming aware of it, can nourish and enrich our inner life. It is up to us to invite the elemental beings to participate in our work and we can thank them for their help and bless them. Through the activity of cleaning, I often feel that I am allowed to create a space in which thinking, feeling and will can develop in a healthy, constructive way.

Tidying and cleaning

On entering a room, I perceive the state of the room and analyse what I see. Is there dirt or cleanliness, clutter or order? This is on the level of earth, and the gnomes help us in this analytical perception.

If the room is dirty, our imagination evokes the image of a clean and orderly room. For this I choose suitable tools and decide for myself where I will start. The imaginative ability and creative connection are properties of water, the world of the undines.

Perhaps the picture of the archetypal purity or the desired order awakes in us a longing for beauty – a process of air and sylphs.

If we are confronted with a mess, at best, it moves us into action, stimulates our will – a fire process of salamanders

Now the work can begin. I decide to create order. Decision is an activity arising out of my innermost self, mobilising the will – fire, salamanders. All things that follow this intent manifest as warmth.

Then comes the real work: scraping, sweeping, removing dirt, all this activity is concerned with the earth element, and gnomes give their aid. The room is dusted and aired. The floor is wiped with rhythmic, harmonious gestures, particles are dissolved in water, water evaporates, and fragrant cleaning materials pervade the room. This is activity of water and air, of sylphs and undines.

Through cleaning, we work with and through all four elements, and thus transform the earth.

In the earth element, we clean, maintain and transform. A dirty bathroom is changed into a work of art, and chaos is transformed into living order.

Water washes, liberates. 'Wash and cleanse me from my sin' comes in American gospel songs. Whenever I was anxious about an exam or had boyfriend trouble, my mother used to say, 'Go and wash it right out of your hair.'

Air cleanses. If we come into a room where a lot of tension is palpable, it can help to open the window to clear the air. In special circumstances, we burn incense in a room after it has been cleaned.

The fire element transforms. Fire rituals in many cultures bring purification, cleansing and healing. If we want to liberate ourselves from old, unpleasant memories, we often burn things connected with them. We may even burn a prayer written on a sheet of paper to strengthen the effect of the prayer through this sacrifice.

Feelings of fear, insecurity, and self-doubt produce a kind of cold that can paralyse the will. Gratitude is a force that can always help us to find the way back to warmth. True gratitude evokes the power of love in us. Gratitude towards the spiritual world warms us and awakens willpower. Enthusiasm and love lead us to action. As Khalil Gibran said, work is love made visible.

The nature of the elements

Earth

The earth is solid and dense and immovable. It is hard, heavy, durable, and it is the foundation on which we stand. It has a firm shape that fills the space it needs. It offers resistance and sustains us.

Each object takes up its space and is self-contained, easy to grasp. This provides stability, security. The fixed laws are immutable: if I throw a stone into the air, it comes down again. The earth absorbs and transforms. The earth works on the roots to nurture and keep plants alive. In its interior it bears treasures – metals, precious stones, petroleum, and coal. It heals through clay or mud packs and mud baths.

When one of her little brothers developed a very high fever that would not come down, my grandmother dug a shallow pit and covered the child with mud, leaving only his nose and mouth visible. Letting him sip water regularly she remained with him by the pit until the doctor arrived a day later. It turned out that her brother was suffering from meningitis. The child survived, thanks to this instinctive act of my grandmother.

But the rigid, solid element may gain the upper hand. Then it can isolate and restrict. The living order may be constricted into an inflexible system. Perfect order and sterility may sneak into the household, expressing an obsessive order. People may become possessive or covetous, even going so far as compulsive hoarding (sometimes called messie syndrome). Such people sometimes show a tendency to hardening and heaviness, which make it almost impossible for them to mobilise their will and order their own surroundings. Lot's wife turning into a pillar of salt in the story of Sodom and Gomorrah is a symbol of someone clinging to the past and unable to let go.

If the earth element predominates too strongly in a constitution, it may lead to illnesses such as sclerosis, deposits and stone formation. In soul and spirit it can lead to heaviness, ponderousness, loneliness or even melancholy.

Water

Although water can easily be put in motion, it forms a final, limiting surface like a skin – a very agitable, sensitive skin. Water moves in ever changing ways; it flows, streams and evaporates. It comes down as rain, forms a creek, stream, river, lake or ocean. It can form a mighty waterfall with mist rising and then become a cloud again. When it gives expression to its natural tendencies in different tones and voices – murmuring, gurgling, rushing or roaring – it reflects a certain similarity with our emotions.

Water purifies and reflects, it absorbs and heals. Healing springs, like Bethesda in the New Testament, as well as spas and mineral baths are found in many places. Near water, we often sense something soothing, relaxing, and even dreamlike; it stimulates the imagination. Perhaps all the water stimulated the fantasies of seafarer's yarns.

Although a spring is often hidden, it can be recognised by the life in its vicinity. Plants grow, animals come to drink, people settle down. In the Namib Desert I once discovered such a small miracle, when between the red dunes I found a verdant green settlement.

Yet water can show strong opposite tendencies. It makes life possible, and in disasters can wipe it out. It rises when it evaporates into the air, and falls down again as rain, striving to penetrate the depth of earth. And while water itself is heavy, we ourselves become lighter in it. Although water takes on every form it is poured into, it also shapes. It defines its path in the river bed, and with time can shape the hardest stone.

Rivers meander across the earth's surface connecting different countries. Settlements and towns come into existence along rivers. And although the river remains the same, it is different from place to place. An abundance of life from the smallest bacteria to the largest plants and animals remain around one place while the water continues to flow. Such a continual flow is also found in the blood's course through arteries and veins of our body. In plants, too, water circulates from the roots through the stem to the leaves and the blossoms.

Water has the tendency to connect and unify, unlike the earth element which tends to consist of particles. Water is very widespread – almost three quarters of the earth's surface is water.

All life is dependent on water. It is the living element itself, and is often called the water of life.

In times of excessive stress people often use expressions related to water, such as, 'I am drowning' or 'I'm in at the deep end,' or even 'I feel like I'm bleeding to death.' In the human body a predominance of the element of water may appear in the form of oedema (the biblical dropsy), or thin blood (thrombocytopenia).

Air

Air is neither visible nor tangible. We only experience it when it is in movement and we feel its resistance. And the movement varies from a draught or gentle breeze to a hurricane. Air has no form or shape, but of itself expands, always seeking the periphery. It can be compressed (even to the degree of becoming a liquid). Different gases can be mixed together without reaching any saturation points.

Air does not hold anything fast, though it carries clouds, birds, butterflies and pollen. Yet it permeates everything, and all living creatures breathe it, it even keeps alive flames. While air has no form, there are occasions when we can get an inkling of the forms of its movement when the air takes on a destructive force as in dust devils, waterspouts, tornados, or even the eye of a hurricane. Some appearances of wind are almost spoken of as beings: the Mistral or Sirocco in Europe, the Trade winds of the tropics, or the Suidooster of the Cape Province in Africa. Through breath and speech man gives shape to the air.

But air can be shaped, as it is when we speak, and it carries our sound. Of itself air has different sounds creating completely different moods. It roars and howls or whispers tenderly. The quality of the air affects the quality of sound.

During a cleaning workshop in a large school, the assembly hall was to be cleaned by all the participants. The hall was very dirty, and had not been cleaned for a long time. Bags of waste were collected, every corner was swept and vacuumed, the floor was mopped and even oiled. The working party had to hurry a little, as the hall was rented out for a weekly choir rehearsal. Just in time we left a very clean hall. No sooner had the people started singing, than the choirmaster came and asked, 'What have you just done to the hall? It sounds completely different in there today.'

The air sustains and revives us from our first to our last breath. When people suffer from exhaustion and illness, a 'change of air' is often recommended. Some countries have climatic spas in the mountains or by the sea where the air is pure. In contrast to the health giving effect of the air, we can experience nervousness and lack of concentration in a stuffy, closed room.

The human body is sensitive to changes in air. Altitude sickness not only causes shortness of breath and various other physical symptoms, but can affect the mind with anxiety attacks. A strong longing to be elsewhere is perhaps also an expression of the air element in our soul. One may become changeable and 'follow any which way the wind blows,' or throw all caution to the wind.

Fire, the element of warmth

The fourth element, we experience as warmth – both externally in our environment and within ourselves. Warmth pervades air and water, as well as the earth. It continually radiates out, striving towards the periphery, towards the heights. In this process it affects all substances it meets, so they themselves may become warmth. In all heat processes live the so-called Salamanders.

Fire is not immediately part of the natural world. It is something that is intimately related to the world of human beings. Animals flee before the fire; they still sense the supernatural force it represents, just as a lightning bolt from heaven and is sublime and terrifying at once.

Greek mythology relates how Prometheus brought it to the earth, against the will of the father of the gods. In earlier times the gods revealed themselves through fire, as when Moses recognised God in the burning bush that was aflame and yet was not consumed. Through trials by fire human beings sought to divine the will of the gods. Burnt offerings were brought as atonement, and the favour of higher powers were invoked. Considered to be a divine gift, fire bestowed power on those who possessed it. This power could be used for good or for bad. In fairy tales, there are positive bearers of this power, like blacksmiths and charcoal burners, dwarves and even witches, and there are negative bearers like devils and vicious fire-spewing dragons.

In our body we can see the element of fire at work in a fever. The body wants to transform what has entered as an alien element. Young children have a slightly higher body temperature than older people, as their body is still changing and transforming.

As soon as we are touched by the first warm sun rays of spring, we drop protective layers and turn towards the warmth, and open ourselves. In the summer we are much more enthusiastic than in winter. Instinctively, we want to connect with the spirituality experienced in warmth. The human being's spiritual core, the self, is experienced in this warmth.

Plants, too, need the element of warmth to thrive and to germinate their seeds. While of course the element of water is required, it is warmth that ripens the fruits.

Outer warmth is closely related to inner warmth. We feel comfortable with people who radiate inner happiness because we feel their warmth, while resignation, indifference and apathy are qualities which express coldness and create distance.

Warmth unites and pervades a whole room. When moving into a new living space, we invite friends and family to a 'housewarming' party. Through the sharing of joy and good wishes, the house is then filled with benevolent warmth.

An excess of warmth or fire, can lead to a fiery temperament showing impatience, anger, irascibility and violence. And if this excess is turned inwards, instead of the spirit of warmth, alcoholism may result. In an inebriated state people do not feel the cold, and time and again intoxicated people freeze to death.

Elemental beings

Throughout the ages in all different cultures we find descriptions of various nature spirits and other spirit forces, called by many different names. The spirits of the air are called elves, fairies, samodives, swan maidens, and many other names. Among water beings we can distinguish nixies, sirens, mermaids, sprites, undines and so on. The beings of earth appear as dwarves, gnomes, pixies, elves, goblins, kobolds, brownies, trolls and leprechauns.

Of course, I had often read about these beings in many different books, but I came across the word 'elemental' for the first time when I started caring for the house of a famous painter many years ago. This lady had to go away for two months. We discussed my responsibilities during her absence, and I suggested that I would give the house a good cleaning after her departure, and on the day before her arrival I would come and clean the house, air the rooms, arrange fresh flowers, so that all could be fresh and beautiful when she came arrived. I was very surprised when she replied, 'Please come every week at your regular time and in your particular rhythm. If you do it differently, my house spirits, the elementals will be wild when I get home.'

If she had many visitors, she would asked me to come in addition to the usual weekly intervals, as she was unable to paint, as she had the impression that the elemental beings needed to be reassured and calmed by my work. This of course excited my curiosity and I started to look into this fascinating subject.

I began to understand that elemental beings are relational beings: they live and act within the human relationship to the world, they represent the relationship between the outer world and our inner self. The more we develop our perception, the more we become aware of these relationships. Through conscious perception our sense of responsibility is strengthened. To give a simple example, if I perceive something that is somehow out of place, do I pass by because it has nothing to do with me, or have I formed a relationship through my perception? Are my gestures then guided by my perception? Does the perception encourage a deed, a need to assume of responsibility?

Elementals are spirits who do not take on a physical embodiment. They work invisibly into the visible; they intrinsically enliven the earth, water, air and fire. As beings of the threshold they always create a relationship linking the spiritual, invisible world to the earthly, visible world. They (especially the gnomes) solidify everything to make it perceptible to humans, thus enabling us to experience it.

An important confirmation of my earlier dream about the helping and hindering beings, was reading of Rudolf Steiner's *The Karma of Vocation*. In this book he talks about how elemental beings come into existence.

> But what is really important is that human horizons should be broadened; that is, that we should learn to know that everything is permeated not just by a single divine spirit conceived in the vaguest way possible, but that spirit is also omnipresent in a concrete, special sense. People must learn to know that when a workman stands at his vice and the sparks fly about elemental spirits are being created which pass over into the world process and there have their significance. Those especially clever ones will claim that this is stupid. These elemental spirits, however, will certainly come into existence even though the one working at the vice is unconscious of them. Nevertheless, they will still be created, and it is important that they shall come into existence in the right way since elemental spirits both destructive and helpful to the world process can come into being.[4]

This is how I first became aware of the great responsibility we have, when we do things. Through our actions processes take place, matter is transformed and our environment is influenced. How we act and with what consciousness we act determines the quality of elemental beings created and their effect on our surroundings.

Once I learned more about these elemental beings it made me realise how important self-observation and self-education was. Even if we do not yet understand this realm very well, and even if we do not perceive these beings, they are nevertheless present. Once we are aware of this we begin to act differently.

Fairy tales

In many fairy tales we hear of house spirits or elemental beings that live under the stairs or on the thresholds of our homes. In the evening a bowl of porridge or milk is placed there as a reward for good services rendered to the home and the family members. This creates a link, a relationship between the interior of the house and outer nature, between the conscious and the unconscious. As messengers of the spiritual world, elemental beings are small guardians of the threshold who sometimes let the invisible pass into the visible.

In fairy tales we also learn that a positive attitude in a difficult situation tends to summon positive, helpful beings, whereas a selfish or victim mentality often summons rather less helpful ones (like Rumpelstiltskin). In Snow White we see that the dwarves like to work with her. They ask Snow White to look after their household – they long for the attention of human beings.

We can learn from fairy tales how images show us what we are often unable to express in words. Just like the fairy-tale heroes, we can learn to follow inner impulses. The boy who followed the advice of the gnome at the roadside found his way to the royal palace. Often there is also a hidden warning to go with the advice, and this then calls for our undivided attention.

The Tale of the Primrose tells of a shepherd who finds a beautiful big cowslip near a rock which he then puts on his hat. The flower turns into a golden key, and instantly a fairy stands in front of him. She tells him that he should put the key on the rock, which will open up to him all the treasures of the earth. The herdsman obeys, and as a grotto opens, he is allowed to take whatever he wants. He gathers together as much as he can carry, but ignores the fairy's warning not to forget the most important thing of all. In his greed he leaves behind the key that had opened the cave to him. The tale ends with the words, 'Since then the primrose does not open the treasures of the earth anymore, and the fairies who had revealed them to people were no longer seen.'

An interesting example is found in the folk tale of the Farmer and his Goblin.

> A farmer had become quite weary of his goblin, because it caused all sorts of mischief, but try as he might, he could not get rid of him again. At last he contrived to set fire to the barn, where the goblin had his home and to burn the goblin with it.
>
> He carted all his straw out of the barn and once the last load was safe, having locked in the sprite, he set fire to the barn. As it was in full blaze, the peasant looked about and, there was the goblin sitting on top the cart saying, 'It was high time we got out of there.' So the farmer had to turn back and keep the goblin.[5]

Elementals and the environment

Some people have a tendency to paint things a little too black, and are of the opinion, for example, that there are no more elemental beings left in cities, in polluted rivers and in monoculture forests. And yet, everything we see, hear, touch or smell is full of beings; even our thoughts are living beings. There are of course plenty of places where we see that nature no longer seems healthy and vital. Instead of feeling revived by nature, we feel the need to contribute something to help nature regain its vitality. As long as trees are still green, some life remains and we can help to revive it. Sometimes we discover a tiny garden or a flower box in a city that looks very much alive and even more vital than a forest, because it is cared for with love and devotion.

It is also alleged that elemental beings are withdrawing and turning away from people. Without their creative service, however, everything would die. Even after the worst disasters it is amazing how quickly nature recovers, especially in places where many people volunteer selflessly to alleviate the disaster. Nature cannot be stopped. Once a house or yard is empty, weeds take over, and soon we see little evidence that once there were vegetable or flower beds.

I do not wish to speak in favour of an uncaring way of working with nature. It is always very painful to hear of another disaster be it an oil slick, dying forests, a bush fire, flood, volcanic eruption or earthquake. Our concern in the face of these disasters must be to have positive and helpful thoughts and deeds that may help avoid further disasters. That includes becoming aware of how we as humans influence the world of the elemental beings.

Schooling our alertness

As long as we have no sense for elemental beings, we can either believe in them or not. But we can begin to develop a sense for them by keeping an open enquiring mind, creating space for answers to come. This requires the hard work of our inner activity and can lead to a more profound comprehension based on experience and not merely understanding some information.

We sometimes experience moments of insight through comments of others, particularly children. When my daughter was four years old, we planted some Swiss chard seedlings in our vegetable garden. The next morning there was no trace of the plants. The slugs had obviously had a midnight feast. I immediately bought new plants and came back armed with some slug pellets. Once we had planted everything I reached for the slug pellets. My daughter wanted to know what I was doing. On explaining, she cried out in horror, 'But Mummy, you can't put poison near the rhubarb. A lot of little dwarfs live there and they like slugs.' The slug pellets remained in the pack.

Taking more conscious note of such moments, refining and developing our attention for them, will help us to become more aware of these elemental beings.

Some mothers know this well. After a long drive to a vacation home and before unpacking, everything has to be cleaned. This often annoys husbands and children, but these mothers know that if they have not worked here, the space will remain alien, or the room may even appear to have a hostile atmosphere. Through cleaning, the room is transformed, and the elemental beings are pacified. My friend's family take a flute or violin with them on their travels so that music can sound forth in every room, before they really feel at home.

During my travels I sometimes have the experience on opening the door of a hotel room that I immediately know that I cannot stay there. It is inexplicable, but I know that there is something unpleasant in the room. We can have a similar experience sometimes if we are invited to a dinner, and the host couple opens the door with wide smiles and warm words of welcome, yet the atmosphere is so loaded that you sense clearly that they must have had quite an argument just minutes ago.

Through my work, I seem to have developed a certain sense that makes me more sensitive to everything around me. Sometimes people ask me to look at a room because they sense something negative in there. They are then surprised if I am unable to find anything. This is simply because I do not have the same relationship to the place as they do. Whatever it is that they experience as negative is neither threatening nor unfriendly towards me.

On the other hand, I notice when someone has created a very nice atmosphere in a room. I feel much warmth and love in certain homes. It is even possible to experience something similar in an office. In big buildings with numerous offices, some offices are so warm and bright that you become aware of a very special quality that lives there. One can almost feel the ideals and spiritual striving of the person who works there.

In a hospice for terminally ill patients, we not only clean the room after a patient has passed away, we also wash the curtains and the wipe down the walls with a damp cloth. This is done not because they are particularly dirty, but to free the space from whatever was linked to the previous patient, before receiving a new patient. One need not be clairvoyant to sense all that has happened in such a room.

The more we practice attentiveness to these subtleties, the more we remember things that we knew instinctively as a child, but seem to have forgotten at some point. How awe-inspiring the world was, and how precious each moment in life was then. Looking back, we suddenly realise exactly why we felt comfortable with one person and uncomfortable with another. Perhaps a feeling or a fragrance triggers our memory, and suddenly it becomes clear why we preferred to stay at the grandmother whose house smelt of baked bread and where we could breathe the scent of lavender while being cuddled on her lap. Perhaps the other grandma's clothes always smelt of moth balls and everything was so clean, so tidy and orderly, that it felt more like a hospital than a home. It felt cold and empty simply because the rooms were sterile, tidied and scrubbed to death.

Through practice we remember things forgotten. Slowly perceptions that were hidden deep within us start rising to the surface. It is very important not to take these first tender perceptions as universal truth, and especially not to proclaim them as such. The first observations do not reveal the whole picture, and can therefore also lead to errors of judgment. It takes time, patience and effort until our partial perceptions fuse with those of friends or others into one truth, into one whole.

The more we become aware of our perceptions and the more we think about them, the more we awaken these dormant faculties. In silent communion with nature we sharpen our perception; we search for the mysterious connection between our innermost being and the invisible part of the elements within us. This is the beginning of devotion.

Different elemental beings and their relation to us

There are many books about these nature beings, about how to deal with them, and even how we can save them from destruction. Rudolf Steiner speaks about elemental beings in a hundred and fifty different lectures. Following these portrayals, I would like to give a short though incomplete description of elemental beings.

In caring professions, these beings can be an important support. In agriculture, in social, educational and healing professions, and especially in parenthood which combines aspects of all these professions, elemental beings play a major role. If our soul finds a relation to the serving, constructive elemental beings, it will also free us from sensationally seeking for knowledge or experiences.

Rudolf Steiner spoke of the importance of our finding a relationship to elemental beings that would help them in their development. One of his fundamental ideas was that all spiritual beings, human beings and nature beings are all on a path of development. Elemental beings depend on the moral behaviour of people, who need to guide them in their development and redeem them, for at present elemental beings have no morality and no conscience.

Gnomes

Their element is the earth and they work invisibly in all tendencies and forces that solidify. One might even say they configure the solid element.

Tradition attributes great wisdom to gnomes. Illustrations some- times show them with a certain similarity with the bird of wisdom, the owl. Legends and fairy tales refer to gnomes as counsellors who reward honest human effort with good ideas and help in solving difficult tasks. However, they punish foolish or conceited people, by granting their silly wishes or by seemingly taking ill-considered statements seriously and following them literally. The hardness of their element can make gnomes ruthless, and their cleverness can lead to derision and being loveless. The solid element offers them no resistance, they swim and flit through the earth element and settle down comfortably within the earth.

They like to form friendships with humans and long for our loving attention. In many fairy tales gnomes are happy helping in a household. Our human task is to redeem gnomes from their one-sidedness, from their tendency to harden the earth element too much, from greed and meanness with their treasure. Their cleverness can set them on the wrong path to evil.

Undines

The water spirits can be wonderful, yet also dangerous. They are capa- ble of great love, but their love is possessive. They tend to draw what they covet into their element, like the Sirens of Greek mythology. In fairy tales they are generous to those whom they treasure. They bestow gifts such as pearls, a special kind of fish, as well as invisible gifts such as catharsis, self-knowledge or insight into the distinction between reality and semblance. Undines weave the gnomes' hard, single ideas into a flowing, contextual thinking.

The spirits of the water element yearn for salvation. Their wish is to transform into another, higher form of being. Their desires sound forth in laments and water music. They can be redeemed through their relationship with human beings or by the helping action of the spirits of air.

Sylphs

Sylphs are also spirits of love like the undines, but their love is selfless, not possessive. Such a spirit of love is Ariel, as represented in Shakespeare's The Tempest or in Goethe's Faust. Hans Christian Andersen (1805–75) tells of the little mermaid whose possessive love turned into sacrifice and devotion, which enabled her to ascend to the daughters of the air.

Sylphs want to connect with people, too. But they are elusive because they do not want to be possessed, nor do they want to possess. In fairy tales, they sometimes assume the shape of swan maidens. Their demands of the human beings are high: to follow and find them is difficult. Yet it is through these challenges that human beings grow and find their own being. Only the are they ready to reciprocate the selfless love of the swan maidens. In short, sylphs exhort us to self-discovery and self-development.

Salamanders

Salamanders, the spirits of fire, are mysterious elemental beings. Fairy tales and legends speak more of the fire element than of the salamanders themselves. Fire beings are created through our benign contact with and loving care of animals. While gnomes bestow wisdom, undines encourage purification and self-knowledge and sylphs promote selfless love, salamanders call on us to recognise the divine will through burning up our illusions. They call on us to use freedom and power – a divine gift – in such a way that God's will is done on earth.

The redemption of elemental beings

Rudolf Steiner offered suggestions as to how we may help or indeed redeem elemental beings. As we have seen, through our behaviour, attitude, character and even our moods we affect the elemental world.

> Look at any solid substance. Once it was fluid. It has only become solid in the course of development. What is liquid was once gaseous, and the gaseous state arose from the smoke that proceeded from fire. But an enchantment of spiritual beings is connected with each stage of densification.
>
> Let us now look at the world that surrounds us. The solid stones, the streams, the evaporating water that rises as mist and fog, the air – everything solid, liquid, gaseous, and fiery – these are all, in fact, nothing but fire. Everything is fire – that is, densified fire. Gold, silver, and copper are densified fire; everything was born of fire; but in all forms of densification, spiritual beings lie enchanted! ... The beings we have to thank for everything surrounding us had to descend from the fire element and are enchanted within the things of this world.
>
> But can human beings help these elemental beings in one way or another? ... Can we release them? Yes, we can. For human actions on Earth are nothing but the external expression of spiritual processes. Everything we do here is also of importance for the spiritual world.[6]

Other nature beings

I would like to briefly mention other beings which Rudolf Steiner describes, but that are not mentioned as often as the nature beings of the four elements. There are also nature beings which let us experience the changes of day and night, the waning and waxing of the moon, as well as the path of the sun and the seasons resulting from it. The spirits of the time of day, of the months and of the seasons are influenced by our attitude and awareness, with which we experience these rhythms, the way we act out of our character traits influences them. There are also helpful beings and hindering ones. I want to tell of a personal experience relating to them.

Invisible helpers and mischievous hinderers

How very wrong people are if they think they are on their own when nobody else is physically present. Most people do not perceive any creatures of the invisible world which surrounds us. As well as elemental beings, there are countless other unseen helpers who accompany and assist us, such as angels and the spirits of the deceased. We must also be vigilant for those spirit beings that are not well disposed towards us and tempt us. Whether benevolent or seductive beings surround us obviously depends on our inner state. Angels and luminous beings may come to visit, or dark creatures may be creeping around the soul seeking nourishment in our uncontrolled, impassioned emotional outpourings. Many medieval painters depicted these beings, such as Hieronymus Bosch, or Matthias Grünewald in The Temptation of St Anthony (part of the Isenheim Altarpiece in Colmar).

Every spirit being needs its own way of being 'cared for'. We cannot always deal with them in the same manner. In a school being cleaned by my company there was a room with an extremely unpleasant smell. I tried everything possible – biological agents, chemical agents – to eliminate it. I even used a steam cleaner to blow into each nook and cranny. Nothing worked: the smell persisted. Thinking that perhaps I had not been loving enough, I tried to be very gentle and attentive to the room and its objects. I even sang at work. Nothing happened, and I believed that I'd just have to live with it. One evening when I arrived at the school it was oppressively hot, and opening the door, the penetrating smell really hit me. I experienced it as a wild animal leaping at me and I became so furious that I threw open the window, stamped my foot on the floor and shouted, 'Now I've had enough of you. I'm here now, and there is no room for both of us. Get out!' I began to clean vigorously, almost punching and kicking the dirt away in a rage. All of a sudden the smell was gone, and it stayed away.

Some months later I passed the care of this school to a colleague. When I filled in for her during an absence, the smell was back. At least now I knew how to go get rid of it. After some vigorous, assertive action the smell was gone again. When my colleague came back, I asked her if she had noticed this smell. She said it had not been there in the beginning, but had gradually become increasingly stronger. I then explained how to deal with the problem, and she managed it too. It does not require a special talent to take care of these spirit beings, only knowledge of their nature, and the will to do something about it.

Day and night

Some elemental beings are imprisoned in darkness so that we human beings can experience the darkness of the night. People who are listless and lazy during the day, do not alter the situation of these beings of the night. However, people who are active and hardworking, devoting themselves joyfully to a task, transform the sacrifice of those spirits trapped in darkness in such a way that they can once again rise to the light.

Our gratitude is the decisive factor once again. There are always reasons to be thankful, even if we are sick or unemployed. We may be active without physically working, perhaps by meeting somebody with interest, or by following world events with awareness. We may become inwardly active and redeem the spirits of the night.

The phases of the moon

The moon and its phases affect our emotions and changing moods. In order to experience the waxing and waning moon on earth a host of elemental beings are necessary, as is the case in the change from day to night. Rudolf Steiner describes that at the waxing moon elemental spirits from a lower world are transported to a higher world. The waxing moon is for them a liberating force. In order to maintain a balance, other beings have to leave the higher regions at the waning moon to be locked into the lower realms. There they are enchanted, as if spellbound.

Human beings have the task of freeing such beings by acting in the same way as the forces of the waxing moon. To do this we have to master and regulate our changing moods. We experience the waxing and waning moon as opposites. While their external appearance will remain, in our soul we can bridge these opposites.

A full moon may cause exuberance and hyperactivity in some people. And for some people the waning moon can lead to depression and passivity, for others it can lead to hypochondria. It is important that we are not at the mercy of such conditions. If we try to practice equanimity an remain cheerful in the face of difficulties, we develop forces that can liberate these beings. It is of course not possible or necessary always to be happy, but we can aim at a generally joyful attitude and mood of contentment. It can become a strength if we are able to have a positive outlook when faced with all the negativity we find around us, for instance in the media. Negativity does not inspire, it leads to resignation and counteracts all power that could bring about something positive.

The seasons

The year may be experienced as a great breathing of the earth. In spring and summer, the earth exhales and we experience growth, blossoming and flourishing: it is a time of liberation. Each out-breath is followed by a contrasting in-breath In autumn and winter the earth takes everything back into herself. The forces of growth in nature cease, as if paralysed. We can assist the elemental beings' liberation by experiencing the year as a breathing of the earth. Without the overview human beings have, elemental beings are unable to experience the light and the dark half of the year as a unity. They are completely immersed in and bound to spring, summer, autumn or winter. However, as human beings we can begin to sense that when the nights become longer and the days shorter, when there is no longer outward growth, then spiritual begins to come to the fore. If we take up this thought into ourselves, we redeem elemental beings. Working with Rudolf Steiner's Calendar of the Soul has greatly helped me to a better understanding of the course of the year. In the preface to this calendar Rudolf Steiner writes, 'The course of the year has its own life.'

Some people no longer know how to create a special festive atmosphere at Christmas or any other annual festival. Rather than drawing strength from the Christmas season, they are caught up in excessive busyness, or else become depressed. The dying of nature around us can lead to inner emptiness rather than to inner light.

To summarise, we can help elemental beings in the following ways:

- ❆ Elemental beings through lovingly perceiving the physical world with wonder and reverence;
- ❆ The beings of day and night through hard work as gratitude for their gifts;
- ❆ The beings of lunar phases through a cheerful, harmonious soul mood;
- ❆ The beings of the seasons through true reverence and devotion to the spirit permeating the world.

These exercises may seem easy, but demand a readiness to observe ourselves accurately. Each of us can learn to take responsibility and participate in the great task of the future development of our earth. Working in this way teaches us to overcome passive resignation and develop confidence to live up to this task. Every positive thought, every feeling of joy and gratitude helps in this task.

The effect of beings we create

'We [human beings] seem born to be dissatisfied. And our thirst for knowledge is but a special instance of this dissatisfaction,' Rudolf Steiner wrote in *The Philosophy of Freedom*.[7] However, if we are discontent for the sake of discontent or because we have fallen into a victim role, it becomes a destructive force. My father used to say, 'Discontent opens the door to all demons.' This leads us to the question, what are demons?

Omraam Mikhaël Aïvanhov once said to me in a conversation, 'There is a stream of life, and there is a stream of death. The first degree of death is discontent. If we are not careful, discontent turns into sadness, even sullenness. This sadness turns into sufferings which can become physical pain. The pain becomes an illness leading ultimately to death. Between the streams of life and of death, there is much misery, suffering and remorse. Contentment and gratitude leads us to the stream of life. They bring us joy which leads to peace, inner calm and happiness. These bring strength and courage, giving us a life of abundance, eventually leading to eternal life.'

When we clean, we are always acting in the social realm. Wherever we are active in social and caring professions, our attitude towards our profession becomes extremely important. In these professions we often feel overwhelmed, and this can lead to burnout. If we are overloaded and overwhelmed, we are not always master of our feelings, thoughts or even utterances.

Rudolf Steiner points out that we have to learn to drive out demons from the circumstances surrounding us. He describes particular beings created by us.[8]

Phantoms are created by vices, slander, lies, convention and coloured truths. They are redeemed by a clear thinking attitude, by feelings of beauty, by good constructive ideas and clear concepts.

Spectres are created by incompetent social institutions that lead to discontent, disharmony and strife that influence people negatively. They are redeemed by social institutions that work in healthy and meaningful ways, by a good and harmonious atmosphere.

Demons are created by an attitude of intolerance, (in our thinking also), by compulsion, obsessiveness or bullying. They are redeemed by tolerance, respect and acknowledging the freedom of others.

The little devil and the snake

Born blind, Ursula Burkhard has written a number of books about elemental beings which she was able to perceive. She also wrote a number of stories, including the following.[9]

In hell, there are regular team meetings. The devils copied this term from us humans. When the team meetings were inaugurated, one of the senior devils gave an address. He explained that all employees in a team are equally important, all have equal rights and obligations, many things would be different from now on, because hierarchical systems are heavenly and therefore undesirable in hell. They talked back and forth for a long time about how much would be new or was new already but in the end, everything remained pretty much as they were before.

The devils of lower rank actually believed that real changes had already come about, simply because the meetings were now called team meetings. They did not notice that all they actually believed in were empty words. They could not even think about what had been discussed, as they were too busy trying to soothe their burning eyes. For on leaving the room the superior devils had put sand in their eyes.

'We have done well,' said the chief devils. 'Human beings continually deceive each other with big, empty words if they want pretend that something is being done. Here and there one can also learn something useful from those blockheads.'

At the regular team meetings the lower ranked devils had to report their achievement on earth to their superiors. Try as hard as they might, the chief devils were never satisfied with their attempts. In hell it is customary to dislike anything someone else does. It would be out of the question to praise the action of a fellow devil. (Praise is, of course, something heavenly, and therefore undesirable.)

One of the smallest devils was always having a bad time of it, whenever he had to report. He was in fact a bit dreamy, and the inhabitants of hell did not appreciate this one bit. Excessive activity is welcome, but dreaming could lead you astray and make you forget your diabolical duties. Things got worse with the dreamy little devil. One day he could not account for any action whatsoever. When asked how he had spent his time, he gave an answer that caused turmoil all around him. He had stolen sunflower seeds from a farmer and chewed on them. In the act of stealing the devils could detect an improvement. But then he had admired the beauty of flowers and discovered that they looked like little suns. He had been basking in the sun and listening to the birds. The thought had occurred to him that everything lives by the sun and glorifies it. The devil concluded his report with 'I had an unknown, but not unpleasant feeling.'

'All we need now is that you preach like a pastor about the beauty of God's creation,' the smaller fellow devils cried indignantly. And the chief devils gave him a severe reprimand. 'You are nothing and nothing will become of you,' they said, 'and if you have nothing better to offer at the next team meeting, we will banish you from hell.'

This caused the little devil great distress. How could he become somebody else so quickly? And where could he go, if they no longer wanted him in hell? Where else can a little devil live? Of course he had to admit that he had not behaved properly. To love flowers and birds is beneath the dignity of a devil. And to admire the sun is totally out of order. Its light often harms the dark plans of hell. The little devil wondered what he should do, turning it over in his mind, but nothing occurred to him. 'Someone must be able to help me out,' he thought. He went to his colleagues to ask for advice, but they all laughed at him maliciously. Helping a fellow devil out of trouble is as unthinkable as to praise him for an action.

Then he went to the animals and asked birds and fish and even the creatures of field and forest. But they all knew nothing of evil, because they lived as ordained by the Creator and according to the laws of nature. Finally the devil came to a wise owl, who whispered, 'Among the animals there is one that has no fins, no wings and no feet. He has already seduced Adam and Eve. Go to him, for if anyone is able to make people living in paradise discontented with what was given to them and inspire them to take what was not theirs, he must really know his job.'

'Why did I not think of this earlier?' called the little devil dancing around on one leg. Then he quickly went to the cunning serpent, and asked him for advice.

'Oh, you silly devils,' hissed the snake, 'You do not quite know evil, but believe it's only through you that it comes into the world. It is all merely an effect.'

'I don't understand,' stammered the little devil in embarrassment.

'I will explain it all to you,' hissed the snake. 'Listen carefully. My poison kills people. Poison has a healing effect, if a physician can properly handle it. So it is neither good nor bad, it depends on the effect. You admire the sun, because all life comes from it. But it acts against life, if it shines too strongly and there is no rain. So everything is neither good nor bad, it only becomes good or evil. You in hell like to arrange some things so they have a bad effect.'

'What about human beings?' asked the little devil.

'They are the same,' hissed the snake, 'they have the choice to act for good or ill, depending on how you deal with them. Only they must not notice that you are dealing with them, for they are just as conceited as you lot in hell. They also believe that everything comes about through them. If they do not notice it, you can influence them in this or that direction. But you can never create evil, although you devils think you can. Once people wake up and truly know good and evil, and they then freely decide for the good, you lot in hell will simply be unemployed. People are not your prisoners as you believe; they are your employers.'

The little devil looked so surprised that the snake tried to help him with further examples. 'If a brother does not forgive the other,' he said, 'something remains between the two which has an evil effect. What grows from this can create work for you, as it lays the foundation for the next evil deed. But far worse than fraternal strife is the evil created when a nation that has freed itself from oppression and begins to oppress their former oppressors. You may then even incite a new war. You don't have to dream it up – it's already there like my poison, a poison among nations. You just have to ensure that it breaks out and takes effect.' The serpent talked himself into fervour, hissing as if licking a tasty morsel.

Thus he spoke his knowledge deep into the little devil, injecting a little snake venom. And what he spoke became a part of the little devil. 'At last one of you silly devils has been so clever as to ask for my advice,' he hissed and dismissed him.

The devil wandered around the world for a long time. He did not want to return to hell until he had achieved something. On his wanderings he came to a small house where a happy family lived. The father, mother and children all had bright eyes, everybody was happy, and everything around them shone like a reflection of their contentment and was clean and shiny. It didn't really take much. The little devil felt an unfamiliar but not unpleasant sensation. He had had a similar feeling before ... when had it been? He remembered the flowers, the birdsong and the bright sunlight, and he got a fright. 'Well, well.' he thought, 'They want to tempt me here. Tempting is my business, though. I must make an effort and try to think of something.'

He shuffled restlessly from one foot to the other, 'How can I go about it?' he wondered. 'I need to change the effect of this gleaming radiance. But how? It is not the sun shining here that dries out everything and destroys life.'

Try as he might, the devil came to no solution, until he overheard the mother say to a neighbour. 'Yes, my dear, everything would be easier for you if you could only be content.'

The little devil danced around on one leg, rubbing his hands. 'I've got it, I've got it,' he said, 'Contentment has to disappear just as it did from the people in paradise, as the wise owl told me. Without contentment, the radiance will be lost. Why, with just a little help from these humans, I'll be able to proudly go home again.'

The devil spat out a little of the poison, which the snake had injected, and smeared it on the things the mother needed for her work – the vacuum cleaner, the broom, the cloths – in short, every cleaning utensil. Then he hid in a safe corner and watched eagerly to see what would happen. As always, the mother began her chores happily. Nothing was too much. She even sang while she worked. But as soon she came into contact with the little devil's poison, her eyes changed. They lost their radiance and she saw only what was wrong, and her face turned grim. She cleaned and cleaned, even where it was totally unnecessary. When the children came home they constantly seemed to be in the way. They could no longer play as before, and were hurt because they were blamed for making everything dirty. Their eyes no longer shone. They lost their love for the little house and the things in it; they no longer felt at home. Then they really did make everything dirty. The mother became restless, she cleaned up and tidied. After a long, arduous working day, the father was looking forward to a peaceful evening at home with his family. But when he came home, he heard nothing but insults, shouts and the loud noise of the vacuum cleaner. Soon his eyes no longer shone, he shouted and grumbled as much as the others.

'The people are playing along,' chuckled the little devil, 'We won't be out of work in hell for some time yet.' He quickly went on his way home. He believed that he had come up something new and was proud of his achievement. Now the chief devils would really be satisfied. In the next team meeting he gleefully told them of his deeds, but was disappointed when the chief devil said, 'Your exile can wait. Perhaps something will become of you after all. You can join the rank of cleaning devils below the ghosts of discontent, on a trial basis. Take good care that your humans don't stray. They might develop a longing for their previous contentment. There is nothing more difficult for us devils than contented human beings. Sometimes the idea occurs to them to transform us into humans and redeem us. I don't know, little cleaning devil, if you could cope with such an onslaught. You'll

*need a lot of strength to defend yourself against these redemption attempts.
I really do not know whether you are strong enough.'*

*The little devil wanted to tell what he had learned from the snake, but no
one listened to him .He was just one of the little devils; the chief devils were
convinced that they knew better.*

Dealing with malevolent beings

As in this tale, the way people feel, strongly influences the atmosphere
in a house and can destroy the happiness of other people. If someone
is grumpy and complaining all his life, this atmosphere penetrates right
into the walls. On three occasions during the twenty-one years of working in other people's homes, I had the experience of being overwhelmed
by what I was confronted with, where I simply had to admit that I could
not go into those rooms. There was a presence of such strong negativity
that I knew that it would be beyond my strength. In one of these three
situations, an old man had cared for his bedridden wife for over twenty
years. But he was an alcoholic and had actually tortured her, rather than
cared for her. I opened the door and was immediately confronted by a
creature that filled the entire room with such negative energy that I felt
very small. Fortunately I did not have to prove my strength to anyone,
so I declined the job.

It is very important to take these perceptions seriously. However,
not everything we initially experience as negative is necessarily so. I
was visiting a house in Norway that was built directly on a rock face. It
was designed in such a way that the floor and one wall of the vegetable
storeroom consisted of the distinctive rock. The hostess asked me to
take a look at this cellar because she only went in there very reluctantly.
She sensed a negative energy and wanted to know if it was good to keep
their food supplies in there. I found an incredibly powerful, elemental
force there, but I did not experience it at all as negative. I was aware,
though, that not everyone would be able to endure such a force.

I told the lady of the house a story I had heard from someone who
belonged to a Chinese family that had practised spirit evocations for
generations. The art was always passed from grandfather to grandson,
never from father to son. During his apprenticeship he accompanied

his grandfather to a wealthy man who suspected an evil spirit in the wine cellar, because the staff refused to go down there to fetch the wine, and every time he went down himself, he found a few broken wine bottles on the floor. The grandfather went through the cellar, speaking quietly to himself, and when he was finished, he made a sign which he hung on the cellar door. The poster read: ' Here lives Wu Li, keeper of the wine cellar.' His grandfather commented, 'The spirit that lives there is not unkind, he is just bored. As I have now given him the task of the guardian of the cellar, he will break no more bottles.' There were no further incidents after that. I later heard that the basement in Norway was no longer avoided either.

Sometimes, however, there are such powerful negative forces, a kind of invisible dirt, that you need special protection to cope with it. I believe this invisible dirt is the cause of the frequent sickness of cleaning staff.

Whenever we encounter a threat we have the instinctive urge to protect ourselves. Some people cross themselves, take out a rosary or a stone, others tarry and say a prayer, or call on a deceased person or patron saint, yet others run away screaming, while some remain trans-fixed, as if paralysed.

I cannot tell people how to protect themselves; ultimately everyone has to find out for themselves. I have an image that helps me person-ally. My four-year-old son was pulling a small cart along a muddy path when he stopped, tipped the little cart on its side, and began to spin the wheels with a stick. The mud flew off in all directions. This image made a strong impression on me. Since then, whenever I felt a strong resist-ance, I concentrate on bringing my 'inner wheels', my chakras, into rotation, and imagine that nothing can stick to me. Our chakras are like turning wheels, and the faster they spin, the stronger are we protected.

Through our work we can change the world. Evil can be redeemed and expelled. I was brought up in a Puritan Church, epitomised by statements like 'knitting on a Sunday is like poking the knitting needle in the eye of the Lord.' This evoked a strong feeling within me of being watched, and that all our deeds were recorded to be rewarded or pun-ished. The fear of punishment was great.

Years later, when I had absorbed more of anthroposophy, it became clear to me that we are indeed watched and what we do or leave undone always has consequences, and that each of us must learn to take responsibility for our actions in life. Through working in a healing way while ordering and caring for our surroundings, we can be open, and invite helping forces, asking them to accompany us in everything we do, and this will, quite naturally, have its effect, and will help protect us from malevolent spirits.

I transformed the horrible images from my childhood, in that I try to say to myself, as honestly as possible, 'Christ is with me, he can and will help me.' I cannot say that I always succeed. There are days when I do not even want to think about it. But deep inside lives the striving to make it possible. When I succeed, fear turns into trust, and my worries are changed into joy. Then the forces that flow towards me help me to transform what I am doing in such a way that I may hope that my actions will beneficial.

> *Christ has no body but yours,*
> *No hands, no feet on earth but yours,*
> *Yours are the eyes with which he looks*
> *Compassion on this world,*
> *Yours are the feet with which he walks to do good,*
> *Yours are the hands, with which he blesses all the world.*
>
> Teresa of Avila (1515–82)

Questions and answers

How can I discover the reason for feeling uncomfortable in a room?
Why don't you ask the room. Simply stand at the threshold, close your eyes and listen very carefully. Try to create an image of everything there is in this room. Be patient, take another good look, and I am sure that you will find the reason. You might even discover something among those things surrounding you which could be important for you at this moment in your life (for instance a document). Perhaps the whole feeling of discomfort came about for the sole reason of finding this object.

A few days after an interview, the journalist made the following confession, 'I really had to smile when you told me that I had to listen to my room. For a few months now I have been feeling very uncomfortable in our living room without knowing the reason. After the interview I went home and I stood in the door as you told me. I had hardly started the exercise when it immediately became clear what was disturbing me. We have a very big wall unit with bookshelves in our living room as the whole family are avid readers. The books had been placed in double rows on the shelves, and this really disturbed me. I started selecting and eliminating some books and immediately felt better. All the members of the family remarked on the change in the room without my having said a word.

In our house we have a very 'strange' room. I have to cross this space to reach the kitchen coming from our entrance, and it always seems stressful just to walk through it. Is there anything I can do about it?
I had a look at this room and discovered a kind of no man's land. This space gave the impression of being a tunnel. It was barely 2 metres across, but it stretched out more than 3 metres to each side. This strange configuration was obviously created when an addition was made to the house; it was like a construction error. The biggest problem was that the space had no clearly defined purpose. It was partly used to store bicycles and other things and there was desk with the PC. When you passed through the space your attention was drawn to this total disorder in both directions. We started by constructing two shelves partly across the openings, creating a corridor between the entry and the kitchen. The shelves left 'door spaces' on different side, which prevented you from looking into both spaces at the same time, creating to two new rooms. These were then tidied and sorted.

What do I do with spiders?
I remove all spiders from my house because they are uninvited guests. At first I also thought they were useful because of the flies and other insects, but afterwards I changed my mind about that. If we kept them as pets, we would have to care for them and feed them, which would mean that we'd have to supply them with flies and mosquitoes! Joking aside, over my many years of cleaning I have noticed that spiders seem to appear when I don't penetrate an area with my awareness. They are often found in attics, cellars, laundries and empty rooms. Even if I don't see any spiders before going away on vacation, on returning there are always a few in the corners. It is also amazing how fast at a house is filled with spiders once people move out of it. Within three days every corner will be filled with spiders.

I used to simply vacuum them, until one day a spider, totally covered in dust and with broken legs crept out of my vacuum cleaners bag as I tried to replace it. Since then, whenever I see a spider when I start cleaning my house I look at it and I say, 'I'm going to start in this corner here and I'm going to work my way around the periphery, and if you are still here when I come to this spot, you risk having a problem.' Almost always when I reached their corners, they were no longer here.

How did you become aware of the elements and the effects they could have on you?
Looking back at the time shortly after the birth of my daughter, I realise how intensely (though still not consciously), I perceived the effects of the elements as well as the elemental beings in times of extreme overwork and exhaustion. Unfortunately, at that time, it was rather their negative effects. I remember experiencing gravity so intensely that it was almost impossible for me to move. Then at times there was a feeling of being dissolved, as if I was bleeding to death, I felt like a puddle of water that flowed in all directions. Added to this was also the strong desire to be somewhere else; to escape, far away from the duties of everyday life, as if floating on air. And finally, the desperate fiery outbursts of anger, during which I once smashed my vacuum cleaner, because my foot got caught in the cable and I had fallen over.

4. Cleaning and the Basic Tasks in Life

Although the title of this book refers to cleaning, creating Starting a cleaning company was but the beginning of a whole series of discoveries. The more I cleaned and learned about cleaning, the more I realised that cleaning covers a vast spectrum of human activity and social interaction.

Caring

Everything we do with love and awareness, reaches a new dimension. When we clean with love and awareness, an enhancement takes place. A cleaned room is transformed into a cared for space, and has an effect on people.

The word 'care' has a range of meanings in English from watching over, to nursing, feeding, promoting development or training. We have all experienced the dulling effect of routine, when we simply do things unconsciously and not quite properly. Things that used to disturb us seem to become part of the surroundings after a while, such as chewing gum stuck under a desk. We no longer quite perceive the condition of our surroundings. Then an unexpected visit is announced and all of a sudden everything has to be spotless. It is like a wake-up call and we finally notice the condition we live in.

Our unawareness not only extends to objects and chores, but also sneaks into human relationships.

Renewal and a fresh start

I have experience how caring for our surroundings even formed the basis for a fresh start. Some years ago, I ran a workshop on cleaning in an adult education centre over five Thursday evenings. I taught various methods, use of materials and tools, but mostly the attitude which could change cleaning into caring. As 'homework' they were encouraged to experiment at home and then share experiences the next time we met. One of the participants, a woman in her thirties, told us that she had been married for fifteen years, had three children and her eldest boy of fifteen had learning difficulties. Her relationship had got stuck in a rut, she and her husband hardly communicated, except when arguing about how to deal with their teenage boy. Five years earlier they had started building their own house which they never managed to finish. Her husband was a handyman who did most of the interior work himself. Because they had both lost interest in the house, it was now neglected, disorderly and dirty. No sooner had she started applying what she had learned in my course, than her husband also started finishing jobs around the house. With an smile she said, 'He actually thinks I am doing it for him.'

I could hardly wait for the next Thursday, to hear how the story continued. She told us how she came home to find the naked light bulb in her hallway replaced with a beautiful lamp. The strings, on which they hung their towels the bathrooms, had been replaced by chrome fixtures. On the last evening of the course, she was radiantly happy and told us, 'My husband has laid all the wooden floors in our house, and last Saturday he decided to finally mount all the skirting boards.' He dragged up all the material and as soon as he started the machine, their eldest son came down and asked if he could help. Father and son worked together for the whole day and managed to mount all the boards. For the first time in months, he had spent Saturday at home and not on the street.

Five years later I met this woman at a conference and she told me that the cleaning workshop had saved her marriage. As both she and her husband started caring for their home again, they remembered all the ideals and dreams they had and the beautiful moments they shared when they started building their home. Her husband even told her it was when she started caring for the home again that he not only felt respected, but he also felt that she was aware of him again. I was profoundly moved when she told me that after working with his father for the weekend, her son had applied for an apprenticeship as a carpenter. He qualified and has developed well since then.

Another workshop participant told me that cleaning could also be the beginning of human relationship. Her dream was to be a social therapist and she was totally happy when she finally found employment in a residential home for difficult girls. She was bitterly disappointed when she was met with indifference, even disdain in trying to relate to the girls. All efforts on her part to form a relationship with these girls failed, and she seriously questioned the soundness of her decision to do this work. She found it very hard to sleep as questions plagued her, until one night she could stand it no longer and decided to get up and do some cleaning in the common areas. This brought her so much relief that she started cleaning every evening after the girls had gone to bed. She carefully cleaned the living room, kitchen and especially the bathrooms. After several weeks one girl approached her and offered to help. Slowly the other girls also opened up to her and she could finally grow into what turned out to be a true vocation.

This is just another confirmation that the love we share in doing our work is an important foundation stone, without which social life cannot truly unfold.

Cleaning with joy

Cleaning is very much a social task. Of course someone who lives alone also cleans to a certain extent, but never quite as nicely as when a visitor is expected. Household chores and especially cleaning are an important part of life and contributes to the restoring and maintaining of a pleasant living environment.

But dirt is not only a cause of human activity, it is also a consequence. Dirt has to do with the past, with something that does not quite fit into the present. I find the definition, dirt is matter in the wrong place, very appropriate. On a field soil is a treasure, but on a white carpet there is no doubt about it being dirt. Removing dirt offers a wide scope for self education and developing new qualities such as patience, attention to detail, perception or perseverance. This activity helps us not only to transform matter, but to develop qualities for the future.

Cleaning is a craft that requires learning. It should be neither a duty nor a compulsion, but it enhances the quality of our life. The joy with which we do this work leaves its imprint on the space. Every space requires care; every room has to be cleaned. This is a chore that is often done without enthusiasm. Whatever the circumstances, we can always try to observe what we do, and more importantly, how we do it.

In the course of a day we have various tasks, some more interesting and stimulating than others, yet all have to be done. This is a fine opportunity for self observation: while doing less interesting things we have a tendency to become tense, we moan and sigh, and often feel that somebody else should be doing this job. Such an attitude only makes things worse. Making a burden out of something exhausts us more than is necessary. We can take a boring task as an opportunity to practice. Taking an interest in every small detail, we might discover something quite new in the familiar. Interest has a reviving quality, and the task at hand becomes less tiring. This interest can lead to insight that can fill us with joy. With joy comes a feeling of strength. If we have been exhausted, being able to experience joy again fills us with gratitude. It is difficult to experience joy and gratitude when we have no energy.

Many people experience cleaning like the task of Sisyphus. The gods condemned Sisyphus to push a huge rock up the mountain, but it always rolled back down. Certain legends claim that Sisyphus found peace when he managed to see a deeper purpose in his task. Crushing situations usually lose their impact once their purpose is understood. Our understanding helps us to become masters of a situation.

We are often brought to our limits and have to face up to our inadequacies through the task of cleaning. We learn to observe ourselves more closely and get to know ourselves better. This effort stimulates creativity and we become more productive. Learning to face and recognise ourselves is an essential step of self development. One of the first steps in self development is to discover where our talents lie. Once found, we have to make the most of them. Our everyday work gives us the opportunity of discovering and developing them. While the result of cleaning is cleanliness, the result of caring is the quality of life and the atmosphere we live or work in.

Art in daily life

Many homemakers and mothers tell me that they don't have time for artistic activity. For many women the mere idea of making time for artistic activity in their lives seems quite far-fetched: there are so many things that need to be done that it is unimaginable to even think of taking time to paint, play music or do some sculpting. Are there not ways of finding artistic activity in daily chores? Is it not possible to turn everything that has to be done repeatedly into an artistic activity? Perhaps we should first choose the art form we would like to practice. Is it singing, painting, sculpting, or acting? Where can we practice any of it?

It is through art, through artistic activity that we become aware of the creative centre of our being. We find it in the balance between our striving towards the ideal, the spiritual world, and the necessities of the physical world. It is from this very centre of our being that we can act in total freedom, and penetrate our deeds with our consciousness. Every conscious act which adds beauty and wellbeing to our family or the community, can thus be considered a work of art. Rudolf Steiner pointed to this in the words:

> What is to be real in the future is borne today within us as ideality. Let us fashion the world so that it will be real. This must not live in us merely as theory; it must be a feeling in us, an innermost life impulse. The we shall simultaneously have a cognitive relationship and a religious relationship to our environment. Out of this innermost impulse, art, too, will become something quite different in the future. It will turn into something that unites with immediate life. Our very existence will have to shape itself artistically.[1]

Honouring beauty

People often feel the need to honour something beautiful. When a girl is wearing a party dress, she usually tries her utmost best to keep it clean as long as possible. Once the first little mishap happens, it no longer seems worth the trouble. I knew a boy who could hardly bear to wear his new shoes, because they were so beautiful and clean and he did not want them to get dirty. No sooner were they slightly dirty, than he felt there was absolutely no reason to clean them after that.

I take great pride in preparing a beautiful table for invited guests. When my daughter turned ten, she wanted to have the table for her party set in exactly the same way as I did it for my guests. I explained that she could then only invite five friends, as I had inherited the beautiful crockery, silver cutlery, crystal glasses and the linen for only six people. She readily agreed and when the big day arrived we laid the table as beautifully as possible with flowers and candles and all the fine things I had. I had kept the dining room door closed until the whole hallway was covered with coats, boots, hats and whatever else. When all were ready I opened the door to festively invite them in. A moment of sheer magic followed. One look at the table filled them with awe, and they wanted to know if it was really for them. I said, 'Yes.' And in a moment these six little unruly youngsters who had left the hallway in shambles, turned into princes and princesses. I served them, and throughout the whole meal they behaved themselves with such dignity and grace that I was even rewarded with a spotless tablecloth at the end of the day (which is more than I could say about my adult guests).

A student from Hungary, who worked with me for about a year, was very keen to learn as much as possible. He especially wanted to learn how to clean the toilets the way I did. He often asked me to check his work and point out any possible oversights. When he came to say goodbye, I told him that he was one of the best workers I ever had and that he had learned very well. He beamed at me and said, 'This is the greatest gift that I will bring home to my wife: having learned how to clean really well.'

On another occasion, a very worried man phoned me and said, 'I need your help. My wife wants a professional to come in and clean for a whole day before her birthday, as a birthday present. Can you believe it?' Not only could I believe it, it was absolutely understandable. More than once my work has been given as a birthday present, and every time it happens, I receive a beautiful bouquet from the birthday girl.

A housemother in a residential social therapeutic setting once told me a lovely story about a very special birthday gift she had received from a young man in her care. He absolutely loved doing the dishes for the whole household. It was his passion, his pride and his joy. He single-handedly washed all the dishes three times a day, seven days a week. On his housemother's birthday, he made her the very special gift of allowing her to wash the dishes, all by herself, the whole day long!

Neglect

Neglect is something invasive. In a very stealthy manner, it starts in all those little corners that we don't fully penetrate. It comes creeping in from underneath the cupboards, from behind the curtains where the spiders make their webs, and from the radiators where dust collects in large bits of fluff. In the kitchen it is often the vent above the stove and the oven that get greasy. Our kitchen aids like the scales which we usually handle with butter and flour on our fingers, often gets stored away as it is. Then there are those special drawers to be found in most households into which every little thing that is not quite identifiable disappears – little notes with numbers, vouchers for special offers, a piece of string or an elastic band.

What do we do, and what do we leave undone? Why do we tend to leave certain chores? Is it because nobody notices anyway, or we simply don't feel like it, or because someone else could also do it for a change?

Henny Geck, a painter who still knew Rudolf Steiner and helped with the carving of the large wooden statue, The Representative of Man, talked about this work. Whenever Steiner was called away from his work on the sculpture he would always sweep up all the shavings lying on the floor and place them in the garbage can. Although she often offered to do this, he insisted on doing it himself. One day she asked him why he took the trouble to sweep up everything even if he had to leave for only a few minutes. His answer was, 'While I am working, everything I work with is part of my working material and I am master of the situation. As soon as I stop working and leave the studio, everything that lies on the floor is waste and therefore belongs in the garbage can. The beings who feel at home in garbage are not the kind of beings we want around when working artistically.'

Homemaking in earlier times

The ten fairy servants

Many years ago in Sweden there lived a family of peasants who had a daughter, Elsa. As she was their only child she was doted upon, and her parents sought in every way to anticipate her slightest wish. As soon as she had been confirmed she was sent to the city to learn how to sew, and also city manners and customs. But in the city she acquired little other knowledge than how to adorn herself, and to scorn housework and manual labour.

When she was twenty years old she won the love of an industrious and honourable young farmer, named Gunner, and before many months had gone by, they became man and wife.

In the beginning, all was joy, but she soon began to weary with her many household duties. Early one morning, shortly before Christmas, there was much activity in Gunner's yard. Elsa had hardly risen from her bed, when the servant, Olle, appeared and said, 'Dear mistress, get our provisions ready, for we are going to the woods, and we must be off if we are to get back before the evening.'

'The dough has risen,' called one of the servant girls, 'and if you come out now, we will have unusually good bread.'

The butcher who had already slaughtered a large hog and several small pigs, had just stepped in to get the accustomed dram, when old Britta came rushing needing the wicks for candle making.

Just then Gunner arrived, impatient because the servants had not yet started for the woods. 'My departed mother,' he said kindly but firmly, 'always prepared everything the night before when people were expected to go to work early in the morning, and I have asked you to do likewise, Elsa. And please do not forget the loom, my dear. There is only a little cloth remaining to be woven, and it will not do to allow it to lie unfinished over the festive days.'

In a rage Elsa rushed out of the kitchen to the house in which the loom stood, slammed the door furiously behind her and cast herself upon a sofa, weeping bitterly.

'No!' she shrieked. 'I will not endure this drudgery any longer. Who would have thought that Gunner would make a common housewife of me

and turn my life into drudgery? Oh, woe is me! Is there no one who can help me?'

'I can,' replied a solemn voice. And before her stood a white-haired man with a broad-brimmed hat upon his head. 'Don't be alarmed,' he continued. 'I came to proffer you the help for which you just wished. I am called Old Man Hoberg. I have known your family to the tenth and eleventh generations. Your family long ago lost its riches, but pride and laziness remained; nevertheless I will help you, for you are good and honest at heart.'

'You complain at the life of drudgery you are compelled to lead,' he continued after a short silence. 'This is because you are unaccustomed to work. But I shall give you ten faithful servants who shall be at your bidding and diligently serve you in all your undertakings.'

With that, he shook his cloak and ten comical little creatures hopped out and began to put the room in order.

Give me your fingers,' commanded the old man.

Trembling, Elsa extended her hand, whereupon the old man, touching each finger, said,

'Hop o'er my thumb,

Lick the pot,

Long pole,

Heart in hand,

Little funny man.'

Then he ordered, 'Away, all of you, to your places.'

In an instant the little servants had vanished into Elsa's fingers, and even the old man had disappeared.

The young wife sat for a long time staring at her hands, but soon she experienced a wonderful desire to work.

'Here I'm sitting and dreaming,' she cried out with unusual cheerfulness and courage, 'and it is already seven o'clock, and outside all are waiting for me.' Elsa hastened out to supervise her servants.

From that day on Elsa performed her duties with as much pleasure as she would formerly have found in dancing. No one knew what had happened, but all marvelled at the sudden change. However, no one was more pleased and satisfied than the young wife herself, for whom work was now a cherished necessity, and under her hands everything thereafter flourished, bringing wealth and happiness to the young couple.

Hands and fingers

Which one of us would not love to have little helpers like that? But what does this fairytale tells us? First, the image of Elsa in her home shows a situation that was still quite common hardly a hundred years ago. It was a time when 'cleanliness is next to godliness' was still a quality worth striving for. Secondly, the spiritual world offers help to those who are 'good and honest at heart' and ask for it. And thirdly, homemaking was still considered a craft that needed the work of hands and even fingers.

Cleaning still is largely manual labour. When we tidy and clean our homes, our hands are our most important tools. Most people love to touch others, animals and even objects they care for. Our sense of touch plays an important part in caring and building relationships. Sometimes a single touch can bring about a transformation, however cursory or gentle it may seem. With our hands we can strike and destroy, but we can also caress, sooth, create or even bless. I shall never forget the gesture of the physician when I gave birth to my son. He held the left shoulder with his left hand while he placed his right hand with a protective, blessing gesture over the tiny head. In later moments, whenever my son was not having an easy time, the memory of this gesture would always comfort me.

It is through our hands that we enter into a relationship with and can transform what is around us. Yet not our hands alone, but the attitude with which we do our work is crucial. We can become aware how, while working, forces flow through our hands, offering something the outside world. Omraam Mikhaël Aïvanhov wrote:

> You leave traces of yourself on everything you touch. And the fact that someone's identity can be discovered by means of their fingerprints and that no two prints in the whole world are alike is ample proof that the hand can express a person's unique character.
>
> Everything that passes through your hands becomes imbued with your emanations and transmits something of the quintessence of your being. When you give someone a gift you are already communicating something of yourself by means of this object. If you live a disorderly life the

object is going to pass on the negative waves you have unknowingly introduced into it, and even if the object you are offering is magnificent and expensive, the person who receives it will not benefit from it. So you yourself are more important than the object you give. Be very aware of that.[2]

During a conference at the Goetheanum I entered a room to clean it, and found the followings words of Rudolf Steiner written on the blackboard, 'When we do not merely grasp with our hand but think with it, then thinking with our hand we follow our karma.'[3] I could immediately see the relevance in everyday life.

If we take a moment to observe our hands while cooking, for instance, we discover the beautiful movements as our fingers 'dance' from one ingredient to the other, or the precise and firm way it can hold a ladle. Notice the flowing movements of the fingers as they arrange flowers into a beautiful bouquet, as they create a colourful and appetising salad, or as they dance over the keys of a piano. Our hands and fingers seem to know what they have to do. Notice too, how our fingers know the password for computer better than my memory: we hesitate if asked what it is, yet our fingers can type it without hesitation.

Creating order can teach as a lot about the economy of gestures, the importance of gesture as such. We can learn that the effect of a gesture continues long after it has been completed. It lingers on in the pain, judgment, rejection it has caused or intended, just as strongly as in the encouragement, comfort and blessing it expressed.

I saw an interesting saying of the artist Dieter Zimmermann[4] on a paper napkin in a tearoom, 'Everything that passes through loving hands, takes on new life.' This echoes the fairytale about Elsa and her helpers, 'and under her hands everything thereafter flourished, bringing wealth and happiness to the young couple.'

Housework today

Often the expectations and role model of a housewife and mother are still based on the social situation as of the nineteenth century. Yet those situations barely exist today, and often all the responsibility rests on the shoulders of the housewife. Though occasionally the man takes on full-time parenting and home-making. Most housewives are also working mothers and this can lead to their being overwhelmed and frustrated. This is often the cause for a deterioration and even break-up of family life.

Depending on the size of the family and the situation, the time spent shopping, cooking, cleaning, doing the laundry and looking after the children can amount to sixty hours a week. This is a task which can lead to total physical and emotional exhaustion. Although family life as such is not often spoken about, cleaning is quite 'in' and is often covered in the media. In Britain two experts Aggie Mackenzie and Kim Woodburn, became TV stars. In the series How clean is your house? they went into different houses to show people how to clear up their mess. The series was a hit and the book a bestseller.

Why do we clean? Why do we bother with their cloth, bucket and broom, when children keep on coming into the house with mud on their shoes and the cat sheds hair every summer? Why bother cleaning the oven, when the soufflé so often runs over leaving a thick black crust on the bottom of the oven? What about the shower with the inevitable hair getting stuck in the drain? Do we do it out of habit, as a sacrifice, or are we all perfectionists? Could it be that we are masochists or compulsive cleaners? What is our goal, what makes us do it, again and again?

A woman once told me that she hates vacuuming and cleaning so much, she only does it when her cat starts having a hard time to get around things. Then she declares war on dirt, sweeps through the house like a fury, knocks off corners, and scrapes the skirting boards, until she drops onto her sofa totally exhausted but with an utterly victorious feeling.

Cleaning means much more than an acquired sense of order, or even a natural need for cleanliness. It is a quality of life that most people need to develop, to be able to unfold their potential. A German psychologist, Elfie Porz, analysed and evaluated the motivation and attitude towards cleaning of her clients. She wrote, 'Cleaning can establish a very pleasant feeling of inner balance. Most people actually enjoy and find pleasure in cleaning.'[5]

Margaret Horsfield describes cleaning as ritual that can take on a religious character, a kind of 'Zen and the art of cleaning'. She also notes that often people tend to turn to their cleaning utensils when they are in a foul mood.

> In a sacred fury the parquet flooring is scrubbed down, a symbolic swipe is taken at the boss's face with a wet rag, heartache warded off with steel wool, or unfair reproaches are swept under the carpet. Cleaning offers the possibility to put our inner disorder into order. The feeling of powerlessness against the chaotic state of the world is alleviated to some degree if we clean up our own house. It relieves our suffering and boosts our confidence.[6]

Cleaning as a profession

Because professional cleaners go to many different places, one might say that nobody knows the condition of society better than cleaners. They not only see what is in drawers and cupboards and behind doors, but can sometimes see into the souls of their clients. They observe a lot but need to be discreet.

Whether in private homes, offices, staff rooms, there are always people who take the trouble to conscientiously clear their desks before leaving work, so that the cleaners can do their job properly. This shows us cleaners that they appreciate our work and therefore create space for us to do it well. But we also find offices that are completely full of things like heaps of old newspapers and magazines that create a lot of dust. We are not allowed to tidy away things, for we are only there to clean, but of course we can only clean where we find the space to do so.

The conditions we find in a house or in an office, say a lot about the people living or working there. Cleaners develop a certain sense concerning their clients. One glance at a desk, into the bathroom, or just touching the surface of a table, and we know whether we are in the company of a chaotic person, a compulsively tidy person or simply someone very messy. However, we come to do our work, not to judge or express an opinion, and it is often part of the contract that we are not allowed to talk about what we see. I was once cleaning the office of the director of a large company. While vacuuming, I noticed that there was a drawer that would not close properly. As I tried to do solve this problem, I discovered that the drawer was filled with empty whisky bottles. As a cleaner, could I say something about it? And to whom should I say something?

There is a retiring generation of cleaning women, now all well over 60 years old, who took great joy and pride in their work. The younger generation of cleaners does not often take the same pride and have the same sense of responsibility. However, in the twenty years of my work with cleaning teams, consisting largely of young students studying at the Goetheanum, I have noticed a recent change. In the last few years there is a different attitude and work ethic among the young people. They want to learn, they want to be of service, and I feel this to be a step in the right direction, a striving towards inner development.

A very regular visitor to the Goetheanum observed the change in the attitude of the young people. He mentioned that some years ago, when he came there early in the morning, he had the impression that the students had a hard time pushing their brooms; they sometimes seemed to lean on them for support. Later he had noticed how the young people were working with a much more upright attitude, with a bounce in their step and were filled with confidence and pride in their work.

Invisible dirt

After construction workers, the profession with the highest percentage of professional disability in Switzerland and Germany is professional cleaners. Why do so many people in this job fall ill? Cleaning can often be an exhausting physical activity that never seems to end. Cleaners are often alone on the job, and they rarely receive thanks or praise. Cleaning is considered an inferior occupation for which no specialist knowledge or training is necessary.

I do not believe that this high disability rate is due only to wrong posture, chemical fumes, fine dust, or similar causes. It may sound odd, but I am convinced that it is largely caused through discontentment, a feeling of isolation, loneliness, lack of mental stimulation and a lack of being recognised as someone doing a worthwhile job. It is not surprising that in the long run this leads to severe depression.

There is also more than just visible dirt. Everything done in a room leaves traces. Difficult meetings, disputes, or even acts of violence or abuse leave a terrible atmosphere in a room. Cleaners having to work in such an environment without any direct relationship to their employer, and who do not know how to protect themselves, are exposed to this invisible pollution and fall ill.

It is demeaning for a human being to work without being able to put their heart into their work. The more they have to do something for which they have no interest or love, the more it weakens their constitution and life forces.

Very often people who clean suffer from a lack of social recognition. However much we may love a clean and cared for space, we very rarely show our appreciation to the people who create it.

One of the cleaning ladies in my company once complained to me that, though she was working in a Waldorf School, people just ignored her and never even greeted her. I suggested she make herself pretty and attend the concert that was going to be held at the school that night. She did just that, and all of a sudden people perceived her in a totally different light. Here was an attractive lady who was interested in music. The following day one of the staff called me to ask when her birthday was. From then on until she retired, she was always greeted warmly and received flowers on her birthday.

Nowadays cleaning has become a very technical business with ever new machines and methods. Most cleaning fairs concentrate on this technical aspect of cleaning. This is of course important to those organising the cleaning, but it does not answer the needs of the people who actually do the cleaning. As well as basic training, they need recognition and appreciation. In many offices and large halls robots are used for cleaning the floors. Of course, we cannot avoid progress, but we need to find a balance between efficiency and human needs. If work is reduced to a calculation of the number of cleaning minutes per square metre, it leads to stress, a feeling of inadequacy, and ultimately to disability. Without a natural rhythm, there is no dignity in such work.

Should we not start to treat our cleaning personnel in a better way? They are the only employees that are allowed to enter almost every room. They develop a comprehensive awareness of the entire space. Whether these people work with engagement and love or indifference

creates a totally different atmosphere and often also has practical consequences. For a cleaner who is engaged and awake during their task
will wonder where the little puddle of water came from that wasn't
there yesterday. They will notice if a surface is unusually damp or if
there is sudden calcium build up on the side of a basin. They will look
for the causes and try to find solutions. In companies where the cleaning personnel work in this responsible and committed manner, they
relate better to the rooms in which they work, and as a result there is
better communication.

Allowing cleaning personnel greater independence and responsibility does not really reduce the efficiency of removing the dirt. As I have
said earlier, if one finds a deeper meaning and dignity in one's work
it will be more economic and efficient. Not only will the atmosphere
improve, the disability rate will go down. Of course cleaning is a very
individual activity linked to the personality. Everybody cleans in a different way, brings different thoughts and feelings into the room, and
through their activity attract different kinds of beings or nature spirits,
which in turn influences the atmosphere of the room.

Awakening a sense of beauty

Many years ago I had an experience that made a profound impression
on me, and showed how caring for a space can contribute positively
to social and pedagogical work. It strengthened my conviction that we
should never underestimate the importance of lovingly caring for our
surroundings.

I was requested to do a thorough cleaning of a residential home for
juvenile delinquents because they were planning an open day. I was
shocked by the state of extreme neglect and filth the house was in. I
could smell the toilets all the way from the basement. I could hardly
see through the windows, there were cobwebs and cigarette butts everywhere, and the door had black marks, indicating that they were often
opened by feet. The stairwell to the three stories was painted with the
most horrific, malevolent pictures in black and very bright colours.

I wanted to know who was responsible for the upkeep of the place.

'The boys,' replied the principal.

'But who teaches them how to clean?'

'The teaching staff do that.'

I then wanted to know if there was an area that was cleaned by the staff, and he showed me the quarters used by people in charge of the night-shift. Of course this was no better, and I told him so. Slightly annoyed he wanted to know whether I wanted the job or not. I said that I was keen to do it, but not with my own employees: I would bring all my equipment and material, but clean the house with the boys and their staff. My offer came as a bit of a surprise. As this had never been done, he had to consult with the board first. I mentioned that the charge would be less than a quarter of that of coming with my employees. Perhaps this had an effect, as it took him less than an hour to return with a positive answer.

As soon as he told me I had the job, I was suddenly filled with panic. I had no experience with teenagers, as my own children were seven and three at the time, nor had I ever seen a juvenile delinquent. And now I was supposed to work with ten of them. So I asked to meet the boys and learn their names beforehand. A breakfast was arranged and I met the ten boys aged 13 to 17.

I now had twelve days in which to prepare myself. My father had advised me on becoming a mother that if I found no solution to a problem regarding my own children, I should address their guardian angel, who knew better than me what their real needs were. So I now tried to enter into a relationship with the guardian angels of these boys. Every night before I went to sleep, I would line up the boys in front of my mind's eye, calling them by their names and addressing their guardian angels. I believed that this was the only way I would be able to get through to them.

As five of them spent weekends with their family at a time, the work was planned for two weekends. Our job was to clean windows, radiators, lamps, doors, floors, showers and toilets. Once they started, they wanted to clean everything. Of their own accord, they started removing (some very explicit) posters and stickers from their walls and wardrobes. One boy felt the need to thoroughly clean his bed, taking it completely apart and in the process finding a whole pile of missing clothes hidden and forgotten underneath it. Another wanted me to show him how he could clean his stereo set 'ecologically'. Of course, they could not work without music; and some music it was. To my ears it sounded like a mixture of an express train and a machine gun. The boy who chose the music told me that it filled him with energy, although I could not see a trace of it. He wanted to know what I liked listening to. I told him that I still liked some of the old sixties music that I used to listened to when I was his age. All of a sudden I heard Cat Stevens Morning has Broken. It sounded like a symphony in comparison to the earlier noise. I was even able to convince the boy that it was easier to clean a window to the rhythm of Morning has Broken than to the 'tu-dum, tu-dum, tu-dum' we heard before.

After a fairly strenuous start, the house was soon buzzing with laughter and joyous activity. It was a wonderful working atmosphere and we managed to get a lot done.

Upon my return the following Saturday, the most wonderful surprise awaited me. The five boys who had cleaned with me previously had with their own money bought white paint and painted the stairwell from top to bottom. But they did not leave it at that. The surfaces were covered with naive childlike pictures: a house with a green door, pink curtains and a smoking chimney; trees covered with red apples and cherries; daffodils and tulips, children flying kites under a beaming sun, and even birds, butterflies and tiny little snails crawling in the grass.

Through the experience of the communal activity of cleaning their own living space, something awoke within them which they probably never even knew they had – a longing for beauty and harmony in a wholesome world.

Curative education or social therapy

When working in curative education, taking care of neglected children, children who have suffered torture, physically or mentally disabled children, cleanliness and order are very important. The same is true in social therapy settings for adults with developmental disabilities. How can children develop in an orderly, healthy, structured way, when surrounded by chaos and neglect? In social therapy settings for adults with special needs or severe handicaps, a cared for environment is essential. Some become quite disorientated or even 'flip' out, if their customary order is disturbed. And just because these people are not able or have the courage to express themselves, does not mean that they are not aware of the situation.

Trainees, people doing community service as well as qualified carers, often clean these institutions. Even where this is not the case, it is always good if everyone working there tries to improve their observation, so that everybody is able to notice any deficiencies and address them.

I often speak to and work with young people who work and live in such anthroposophical residential institutions for children or adults. Many come because they feel the need to be useful and to be of service to people, others come to learn a new language, and yet others come because they need to be part of a family and learn what their parents did not teach them.

These young people often tell me that their sole duty is to take care of the residents and to take interest in their well-being. As a well cared for environment is very important and contributes to well-being, it is true to say that taking care of the living spaces is an extended form of taking care of the people themselves. A home is like an extension of our body.

In my experience most young people are very open to these ideas, and only have to be made aware of them. They come to these institutions, without any idea or practical experience of cleaning and looking after spaces. They don't know how to clean a toilet or a bath, they know neither the cleaning products nor the tools needed. For the person in charge of the house it can initially be quite tiresome, requiring a lot of patience and understanding, to introduce newcomers to these tasks. It is best if young people are introduced to the subject of cleaning and caring as soon as they arrive. Standards of cleaning vary, and this can cause tensions within a community; it is easier to address the subject right at the beginning, stating that in this house we are trying to maintain a certain standard. But of course, newcomers will not know how to reach and maintain the standard. This requires good and patient explaining and practical demonstrations. It may help to speak about the deeper meaning of cleaning.

My work in such residential social therapeutic settings, have enriched my life with wonderful and profound experiences.

During a lecture to tour in America a young woman in such a community asked if I could help her with her room. It looked as if it had been hit by a bombshell. There was not a free inch of space on the floor, a large suitcase lay open with a mixture of clean and dirty clothing stuffed into it. The bed wasn't made and there was a very strong and unpleasant odour in the room. This young, woman (who was also overweight) was totally overwhelmed because she had never been away from home and had never needed to do any-thing for herself, and to top it all she was suffering profoundly from homesickness.

We started by sorting out her laundry: dirty laundry was put into the basket and the clean laundry was neatly placed in the cupboard. That enabled us to put away the big suitcase creating more space in the room. Then we started looking at everything else lying around on the floor. We filled two large garbage bags with rubbish, empty containers, dried out flowers and food leftovers. For the first time in three months her bed was made with fresh bedding. We then cleaned the windows, dusted the whole room with a damp cloth, and cleaned the floor. After little more than an hour not only the room, but also the young woman, looked totally different. She was standing erect and her eyes were sparkling.

I suggested that she should never change her clothes in her bedroom, but do this in the bathroom, putting the used laundry directly into the laundry basket that was right there. In the evening, before going to bed, she should take a close look at her whole room and ask herself whether it looked the way she would like it to be.

This experience shows how important it is for the houseparents, or those responsible, to also be aware of the well-being of younger co-workers. Six months later I received a letter from the housemother, telling me that not only had this young woman kept her room in perfect order, but that she had lost 12 kg (26 lb) in weight.

It can of course also happen that a houseparent can become totally overwhelmed with the situation, without others in the community being aware of it. So it is important that everyone working in such settings observes their colleagues and fellow co-workers and notice if someone becomes quiet, withdrawn, or always has some kind of excuse for no longer receiving guests.

When it comes to adults with special needs, we need to learn how to support and teach them to do their chores. It is helpful to discover where their strengths lie and to concentrate on these. Some like washing the dishes, others like sweeping and mopping, some like to create order in rooms and some even loved to clean the bathtub. It often requires a lot of time and patience to teach them but if they learn to do something well, they have not only gained a skill, but have grown in dignity and the community has also benefited.

I once observed a young man who was wiping the table after supper. Most of the left-overs and crumbs landed on the floor, the surface was covered with smears and the corners were untouched. The young trainee took the cloth from him when he finished, saying, 'Thanks, John, you did a good job.'

That was completely untrue, and I told her so.

'I can't possibly hurt him, he can't do it any better,' she said.

I asked whether she has ever tried to show him how to do it better. She admitted that she had never thought of that. I then addressed John and asked him whether he would like me to show him how to clean the table properly. He was quite willing, and I demonstrated step by step how it could be done, following an precise sequence, using harmonious and decisive movements. He tried it and after I corrected a few of his movements, he managed to clean the table properly.

'Now you have really done a good job, John,' I said, and he beamed with pride.

Since then I have heard that he is still doing well. He doesn't do a lot of other things in the household, but he does clean all tables and other flat surfaces, as well as windows.

I had a similar experience when I tried to teach Paul how to clean the basin in his bedroom. He shared his room with another young man, Albert. In the basin there were lots of Paul's dried toothpaste spots, calcium residue and some odd hairs. I tried to teach him and while I was doing so, Albert was observing us very closely. Whatever I tried to do, Paul didn't seem to understand what I meant, and after a few attempts the washbasin didn't look much better.

After a while Albert said, 'Let me do that. Paul can do the dusting. I don't like doing the dusting.'

And sure enough, Albert learned very fast and did a good job. I then showed Paul how to do the dusting. Here too, he needed a lot of time and a lot of repetition before he was able to understand the system of going progressively from object to object along the walls of the room, and then do any remaining objects, in order to dust every piece of furniture thoroughly. (I taught all my employees this sequence. Start at the door, go either left or right along the periphery, dusting each object or piece of furniture from the top down).

On a visit to the same community four years later, the houseparent told me that Paul has developed into the dusting specialist of the community. He now went from house to house and dusted a different house every other day. It was with pride and joy that he placed his new skill in the service the whole community.

My company was once requested to do a thorough cleaning of a large house in a social therapeutic community during the summer vacation when all the residents were away. As I went through the whole house delegating the jobs, I discovered a toilet which had a strange atmosphere. It was somehow hostile and I could feel a strong resistance. Having found everyone a suitable chore I decided to tackle this toilet myself.

All four walls were tiled from the floor to the ceiling and the door was covered with a thick coat of oil paint. A shower-head was attached to the faucet of the basin. I started cleaning and immediately sensed the strong resistance that I had felt on entering the room at first. I started at the very top cleaning every square inch with close attention. When I reached the surfaces below my knees, I knelt down to do the rest in this position. The space was no bigger than about a square metre and yet I needed more than six hours to clean it before I could feel that the resistance had been overcome.

About three weeks later I met a co-worker from this community and asked her what the story was about this toilet. She told me that it was used only by one seventeen-year-old autistic girl. Every day she smeared the walls with excrement. Every time this happened the walls as well as the girl were washed down with the shower. The co-worker seemed to reflect a moment, and then said, 'Now that you ask me about it, we noticed that on returning from our holiday the girl didn't smear the walls for about ten days. But then it started again.'

I was moved by this information, and it became clear to me the kind of special care I had given this space needed to be repeated. Doing it just once was not enough. Just like a plant has to be watered regularly, difficult spaces like that have to be cared for very conscientiously on a regular basis.

I told this story during one of my seminars at a school in England. There were some co-workers from a neighbouring social therapeutic institution who were fascinated by my story, and they asked me whether I could also visit their school sometime soon in the future. Three years later I finally got there, and the co-workers who had been at my workshop told me the following story.

A young autistic boy they were responsible for had a habit of smearing in his bedroom with excrement every day. They had tried everything without success. They had discussed it with the parents, spoken to his doctor and tried to involve him when they cleaned the room, but nothing changed. After having attended the workshop they tried to change their attitude while cleaning and tried to transform the room. It took a long time for the situation to improve, but now after three years they were able to tell me that the young boy only very rarely smeared his room, for instance when his parents brought him back after the holidays.

On another occasion I was asked to teach all members of each household, including the people in need of special care, of a social therapeutic community. I noticed a young man who was very restless and loud, and was continually accompanied by two men. I was told that this sixteen-year-old autistic boy had times when he would not sleep, and had a tendency to harm both himself and others. For this reason he had to be accompanied by two people 24 hours a day. As the physicians had noticed that these bouts recurred more often with medication, the community was trying not to use sedatives with this young man.

On the day his house was to be cleaned by all he had not slept for three full days and two nights. I looked into his room, and standing at the threshold, I sensed the strong resistance I had met before. I noticed that under his bed there was a very strange kind of dust unlike anything I had encountered before. The dust seemed to be deep, flaky and somehow very lively, almost as if it was moving. Once everybody was busy with their particular chores, I started cleaning his room.

With a damp cloth I wiped the ceiling, walls and all the furniture. I cleaned the windows and carefully vacuumed all the dust from under his bed. I added a few drops of rose oil to some water, knelt down, took a cloth and started wiping the floor down using very deliberate and rhythmic movements. I slowly moved backwards towards the door on all fours and spent a few moments removing the last traces of resistance from the threshold.

'Now,' I thought to myself, 'the room is free of resistance and filled with light.' At that very moment people were calling out warnings, a door slammed and objects were being thrown around. The boy had managed to elude his guardians, come charging into the house, pulled off his boots without stopping, and thrown them against the wall. Everything happened so fast that I was still on all fours in front of his room when he leapt right over me. He threw himself down on his bed, folded his hands on his chest and within seconds was fast asleep. He slept for 22 hours without moving once. It appeared that he was able to find peace in his room now that it had been thoroughly and conscientiously cleaned.

While staff at these institutions have to cope with increasing administration due to many different restrictions, rules and regulations, it is important not to neglect the care of living and work spaces. The time invested in the care of these spaces is amply returned by the improved conditions and relationships between the different members of the household. A house that is lovingly cared for has a healthy atmosphere. Often, if I noticed a particularly well cared for home in one of these communities, I was told that the most difficult residents lived in this house. It somehow seemed to be impossible to look after them in another house.

Questions and answers

Could you explain why my husband and children so often seem unwilling, to help me with the household when I ask them?
Don't ever ask anything of your children or your partner when you are feeling frustrated, discontent or angry. It is better to ask at a time when you are calm and you may find a more positive response.

We all know what happens if over a long period we don't say anything about what actually annoys us. One day some minor thing happens, and our pent-up frustration and anger pours out in a destructive way. The unfortunate subject of our eruption is totally caught by surprise, becomes defensive, and then nothing is achieved. It is wiser to speak when we were calm, or better, immediately after something happens the first time.

But I find that often not much changes. How can I manage to bring about a more permanent change in the situation?
At home or in some public space try making a conscientious effort to care for something, for instance just picking up a bit of litter. The awareness and striving goes into this simple act is what will bear fruit. Keep trying, and trust that something will change in people's attitude. You cannot change them, but you can inspire them to make a change out of themselves.

Are you able to explain to the people with whom you work about communicating with the room?
When I teach personnel in the company or at places where I work, I hint at it, but I don't but I don't ram it down their throats. People have to be open for questions such as these. At the Goetheanum people know about me, and they come to me with questions such as these. When I started working there most people just came to work because they needed to earn money. After some years, people still needed money and wanted to work with me, but they wanted to learn more about the way I worked. This made everything much easier.

I had a total different experience in the clinic where I now work. The sixteen ladies on my team had never heard of me and had never asked for any changes, and then I came. I had been asked to introduce my way of working because the clinic's management wanted the cleaning patients' and other rooms to be an integral part of the therapeutic work. I worked very hard to find ways of teaching them to do things differently. They did not always understand why – some had worked there for over thirty years and were not interested in changes. Yet now, after fourteen months, I do notice a change.

Why doesn't anybody ever thank me or praise me for the housework I do?
When all goes well, our partner and children take it for granted to have

a nice home. Of course, it is nice to receive praise every now and then, but this should not be the reason that we do our work.

A friend of mine had thoroughly cleaned her kitchen and really worked the whole day with joy and dedication. The next morning when a husband came into the kitchen for breakfast he noticed that the window was dirty. She was profoundly hurt because the only reason that she had not manage to clean the window was because it was too dark when she wanted to do it. But actually, her husband's remark was nothing but a hidden compliment. When the whole kitchen was dirty he had not notice the window, but now when everything else gleamed so nicely, it stood out like a sore thumb.

I am very fortunate because I am able to be a full-time homemaker and mother for my two young children. Yet I often miss the gratitude and the recognition from my husband. To him it as totally normal that I do all that I do. I can't understand why he doesn't sometimes at least offer to help me with my chores?
My answer might not suit everyone. Yet I would like to ask you, do you help him with his work, or do you consider it natural that he works the whole day to support his family and enables you to do your job full-time? Have you spoken with him about it? In which way do you wish him to help you? It is important to express a need clearly, because he might not even know that you would like him to help you.

It always surprises me, how fast the tables in the canteen in our clinic become dirty. People leave leftovers and other things just lying there, and after every break I need a lot of time to clear up. Is there any way to solve this problem?
Perhaps you can try it with a nice tablecloth and a little flower arrangement? My experience has showed that people instinctively try to honour beauty. It often makes people more aware, and can inspire them to be more conscientious in the way they handle things and the way they leave things behind.

How do you actually go about cleaning and caring for places the way you do?
I simply try to connect with the room and the objects that surround me with devotion. I try to observe everything around me and also of

myself. Cleaning and caring can really help us to develop our sense of perception. We cannot clean room properly if we look at it through clouded eyes. The reason that so many rooms are badly cleaned it is because people do not really see what needs to be done.

Do you believe that people are able to perceive your particular attitude, and does it make a difference to those who perceive it?
I don't look at myself when I clean, but people have told me that there is a certain devotion in my gestures, and that even just being in the room and looking at the way I do things, seems to have an effect on people and on the room. I cannot judge that myself. A woman once told me that although she had never seen or met me, I had changed her life three years earlier. Her husband had visited one of my workshops at that time, came home and showed her how I cleaned. From that day on everything had changed in her house.

How do your workshops and lectures differ from other lectures and workshops?
I don't really know. Did you find it any different? Every year I give a seminar at a college, mostly for women who want to take up their former profession after a time out with their family. The person who invites me to do these workshops told me that when some well-known people come to give lectures it often leave these ladies feeling totally discouraged – they can't possibly read yet another book, and that the standards are simply too high. After I teach, they don't feel the need to read another book; often they can't wait to get home to simply try it out – and they have immediate results.

   It is no longer only women who are interested in these questions, I have a lot of men coming to my workshops as well.

Do you believe that people can discover in these everyday chores a spirituality which they never thought to find there? Or how can you explain the interest that people take in the way you talk about cleaning?
People are looking for something real, something they can do. When we clean there are so many different possibilities to do little exercises that we can repeat in a regular way. Every day we can do it again and again with awareness and commitment. Something as simple as wip-

ing your face and cleaning the washbasin every evening before you go to bed, could start you on a spiritual path. And it is a wonderful feeling to get up in the morning and be greeted by a radiantly sparkling clean basin without any traces of dirt or hair from the evening before.

Could you tell us something about how different activities which take place in rooms influence the atmosphere of the room? How would you describe the difference in atmosphere of a hospital or a school, a living room or an office?

I discovered something very interesting soon after I started working at the Goetheanum. As I mentioned, it is a big conference centre and conferences relating to many different professions take place there every year. In the beginning I did not know the sequences of these conferences, but whenever I arrived at my work at 6 o'clock in the morning, on entering the toilets, I could immediately tell what kind of conference was taking place at that moment. Every profession has its own qualities and I was able to sense something of them in the way I found the toilets in the morning.

I would notice it in very small things, like what people did with the cardboard tube when a roll of toilet paper was finished. Did they place a fresh role in the fixture, on the bin, the sill, or even straight on the floor? Was the empty tube put in the garbage bin, simply dropped on the floor, or placed on the sill? Why are the floors splashed with water around the washbasins during another conference? At some conferences coffee cups are left all over the place.

I was intrigued that in a hospice, in a room with one bedridden, dying patient, more visible dust accumulates in a day, than it in a kindergarten where 30 children play all day. And the dust is different in every room, according to the illness the patient has.

Sometimes workplaces and offices can become a little bit too homely, filled with a hotchpotch of knick-knacks, photos, or too many flowerpots. Some people even seem to store personal items in their office, perhaps because they have no room left at home. All this must have an influence on the working atmosphere. (People should look at you're their workplace through the eyes of a cleaning woman from time to time.) Fortunately there are always some people who leave their office and desk neat and tidy before they go, and this makes it easier for us to do our job properly. The state of an office can also tell you whether cleaning is important to its occupant or not.

You tell so many stories, can't you just answer the question straight out?
Almost always when people ask me a question some experience I have had comes to mind. I then relate it and often find that the questioner can relate to it immediately, and is helped more by this than by some kind of intellectual explanation.

Why are so many people reluctant to make their bed?
The next time you get up, take a close look at your bed. We don't really hesitate to make our beds because we find it tiring, but because of what it mirrors when we look at it. Our beds are intimately related to us and usually radiate what was experienced during the night. What happened in your bed the night before? Which thoughts haunted you while you tossed and turned without sleeping? When you went to bed were you angry, worried, discontented, or unhappy? Did you spend half the night crying? Sometimes you get out of bed and want to leave everything behind you, other times you have the need to strip the bed and make it up with fresh bed linen even though you did it just a day or two ago. Then there are times when you want to gather all the bedding into your arms, having it close to your heart and inhale the lingering fragrance of the person you spent the night with. All this influences what you do with the bed. Of course many other people get out of bed, and without a second thought, make it.

Why do I find it easier to clean up and create order in my workplace than at home?
At work you are always more objective about what you see. At home you are confronted with yourself and your family. Often you reproach yourself when you realise all the things that you have intended to do, and have not yet done. This can even cause feelings of inadequacy and the mere thought that it is going to be the same again tomorrow can be quite a depressing.

Why do socks always seem to disappear?
I have my very own theory regarding this matter. Washing machines eat socks.

You mentioned invisible dirt that professional cleaners have to deal with. Does this also apply to the private home?
Unfortunately, yes. Quarrels, impatience, jealousy, anger, suspicion, criticism – all our emotions and our actions leave traces in a room. People sometimes come home exhausted, take their clothes off and then just leave them in a heap on the bedroom floor. What caused the exhaustion? Was there a meeting where difficult decisions had to be made? Did someone hurt you, or make you furious? All these emotions still cling to the clothes left lying on the floor. Do you want to sleep in that room? Some people have a desk in their bedrooms covered with unfinished business, and are then surprised that they wake up feeling tired in the morning.

The dirty dishes in the kitchen, empty beer bottles in the living room, the wet towels on the bathroom floor; all these things influence the atmosphere and the way in which you start your day the next morning. Do you want to be confronted with yesterday's unfinished business, or do you want a fresh start? How will that influence the rest of the day?

You spoke about doing and leaving things undone. Could you explain that a little bit better please?
It is important that every person discovers their own individual needs and the conditions according to which they wish to shape their daily lives. Every person has to let their initiative guide them in the steps they have to take, the decisions they have to make, according to what they consider right for their personal situation.

We tend to do many things without really thinking about them. We leave things lying about, sometimes leave doors and drawers open, or take a pen with us after using it, although it doesn't belong to us. At times we do not feel quite right about what we do, like leaving dirty dishes around, or whatever. Sometimes we speak about things that do not really concern us, or criticise without reason.

Repeatedly doing things we do not truly support, leaves traces in our soul that may eventually cause us to be morose, fractious or discontent. In time it may even affect our health. Honest introspection, the will to change and perseverance can enable us to transform an idea into an ideal and give us the strength to act accordingly. This approach will slowly lead us to recognise the connection between perception and morality, between thinking and the sense of responsibility.

5. Spirituality in Daily Life

Hestia

The Greek goddess Hestia was the virginal daughter of Cronus and Rhea. Zeus accorded her eternal virginity and entrusted her with the honourable task of guardian of the home.

Interestingly, there are no known centres of worship dedicated to Hestia and there are hardly any sculptures or images of her (other than being depicted in some Athenian vase paintings). She was traditionally represented by a lamp with an eternal flame.

The hearth was the sacred centre of domestic life, and Hestia was its goddess, bestowing domestic happiness and blessing. Worshipped mainly by the common people, Hestia filled the house with harmony and peace. Her radiant warmth made a house into a home.

Her sacred duty of spreading harmony was so rewarding that she needed neither praise nor gratitude. Certain customs and rituals were devoted to her. A newborn baby would be carried around the hearth after five days. This ritual was followed by a festive meal to integrate and acknowledge the child as a full and worthy member of the household. Hestia's flame was never allowed to go out. Whenever a new settlement was founded, a flame from the old village was taken to the new one.

As a hearth goddess, Hestia was also known for her hospitality. If a stranger came calling and seeking sanctuary, it was considered an offence against Hestia to turn the person away. Those who followed her were obliged to provide shelter and food to anyone truly in need. It was also emphasised that female guests given sanctuary were not to be violated -- again, a grave offence against Hestia.

The religious element in daily life

Nowadays many people have turned away from church religion. But family and society benefit if we are able to discover something sacred in our everyday deeds and activities. Household work and even cleaning present us with opportunities to practise devotion and reverence. For instance, we can try to picture where our food comes from, or all the things that need to happen for a carrot to grow or spoonful of honey to be produced. Saying a grace or blessing a meal expresses something of our reverence for the world around us. In Turkey, people address the person who prepared the meal with a beautiful phrase, 'May your hands remain healthy.' This creates an atmosphere of gratitude.

A sacred attitude towards daily chores is nothing new – we simply have to rediscover it. A wonderful example can be found in a prayer by St Therese of Avila (1515–82).

LORD OF POTS AND PANS

I do not have the time to be a saint and hold
    vigil through the night to please you.
Make me a saint who prepares meals and does
    the washing up.
Prayer time will be over until I have done the
    dishes after supper.
Lord of pots and pans, please, rather than
    winning souls for you,
Let me offer the tiredness that come over me
    at the sight of coffee grounds and burned
    vegetable pans.
Remind me of all the things I am apt to forget.
Not just to save my feet, but that my perfectly
    set table may be offered as a prayer.

Such an attitude is gaining more recognition today, judging by all the books and articles we can find on the subject of spirituality in daily life. A prayer of the early eighteenth century covers the same subject.

THE ELIXIR

Teach me, my God and King,
In all things Thee to see,
And what I do in any thing,
To do it as for Thee.

A man that looks on glass,
On it may stay his eye;
Or if he pleaseth, through it pass,
And then the heav'n espy.

All may of Thee partake;
Nothing can be so mean,
Which with this tincture (for thy sake)
Will not grow bright and clean.

A servant with this clause
Makes drudgery divine;
Who sweeps a room, as for Thy laws,
Makes that and th'action fine.

This is the famous stone,
That turneth all to gold;
For that which God doth touch and own,
Cannot for less be told.[1]

Mindfulness and acts of devotion are essential parts of the Buddhist path. In many other cultures you find a similar striving to raise the mundane everyday to greater heights. In *The Prophet,* Khalil Gibran wrote about the importance of love when you work.

You work that you may keep pace with the earth and the
soul of the earth.
    For to be idle is to become a stranger unto the seasons,
and to step out of life's procession, that marches in majesty
and proud submission towards the infinite.

When you work you are a flute through whose heart the whispering of the hours turns to music.

Which of you would be reed, dumb and silent, when all else sings together in unison?

Always you have been told that work is a curse and labour a misfortune.

But I say to you that when you work you fulfil a part of the earth's furthest dream, assigned to you when that dream was born.

And in keeping yourself with labour you are in truth loving life.

And to love life through labour is to be intimate with life's inmost secret.

But if you in your pain call birth an affliction and the support of the flesh a curse written upon your brow, then I answer that naught but the sweat of your brow shall wash away that which is written.

You have been told also that life is darkness, and in your weariness you echo what was said by the weary.

And I say that life is indeed darkness save when there is urge.

And all urge is blind save when there is knowledge.

And all knowledge is vain save when there is work.

And all work is empty save when there is love.

And when you work with love you bind yourself to yourself, and to one another, and to God.

And what is it to work with love?

...

It is to charge all things you fashion with a breath of your own spirit.

And to know that all the blessed dead are standing about you and watching.

...

Work is love made visible.

What transforms work into an act of devotion? How can work be turned into a sacrament and what does that mean? Ritual links the spiritual to physical substance. Everything we do can become an act of devotion, a service to humanity, a service to the higher worlds. The reverend attitude to work fills us with strength, and can have a healing effect like a blessing, wherever we are, and whatever we do, whether working with people or working in nature.

With such an attitude we receive strength, and we can give strength to others. I once attended a course about the preparation of biodynamic compost. The farmer taught us how all the kingdoms of nature – mineral, plant and animal – contributed to the compost heap. And then the human being fertilises it with spirit, with the thoughts that accompany the stirring and the spreading of the preparations over the gardens and fields. I observed a farmer once very early in the morning, spreading the preparation with rhythmic and harmonious movements over his crops. It was as if witnessing a profoundly sacred act.

Our devotion to small things can always be considered a part of our spiritual development. We can learn to totally surrender ourselves to what we are doing, to the object of our attention. And because most things usually serve human needs, we basically serve human beings through caring for things. If we want to take particular care of a room or an object, it is essential that we perceive it precisely. For instance, take a close look at the legs of a grand piano or a beautifully carved piece of furniture. Have you ever realised how many different surfaces, edges and trimmings need to be dusted? Through our interest in the things we handle, it is amazing how much we can discover.

When working with human beings, we can try to understand them and meet them with compassion rather than judgment. This is especially important if we try to help someone who has lost the ability to create order. Paying attention to everything that surrounds this person can help us to understand how such a situation could develop. Being able to help in such a situation can fill us with gratitude, and that in turn radiates joy and health.

There is a Bulgarian fairy tale, A Samodiva Takes Care Neither of House nor Child. One sentence caught my attention, although many people seem to read over it. A young shepherd observed three woodland fairies, or samodivas as they are called in Slavic folklore, swimming in the lake. After swimming they put on their samodiva dresses and flew away. The next time he was able to hide one of the dresses while they were swimming. This enabled him to take one of the samodivas home to be his wife. She warned him insistently that a samodiva would not take clear of house or child. And then there is this sentence: 'after she had been received by the shepherd's mother she bestirred herself and started making order, and her presence radiated through the whole house. The mother and her son were filled with joy, and none were happier than they.' Is it not noteworthy that her first deed as a human being was the care of the house that filled it with light?

In earlier times, it was a custom in many parts that a mother would rise early in the morning and speak a blessing as she lit a fire in the hearth. Alexander Carmichael (1832–1912) wrote down and translated the prayers and blessing he heard in the Highlands and Islands of Scotland. On the Island or North Uist he heard a crofter's wife reciting these words.

> I will kindle my fire this morning
> In presence of the holy angels of heaven,
> In presence of Ariel of the loveliest form,
> In presence of Uriel of the myriad charms,
> Without malice, without jealousy, without envy,
> Without fear, without terror of any one under the sun,
> But the Holy Son of God to shield me.[2]

The way in which Rudolf Steiner spoke about deeds of love made a strong impression on me.

> We owe our existence to acts of love done in the past. The strength with which we have been endowed by these acts of love is the measure of our deep debt to the past, and whatever love we may at any time be able to bring forth is payment of debts owed for our existence ...
>
> Let us think of the meaning and effect of love in the world in the following way. Love is always a reminder of debts owed to life in the past, and because we gain nothing for the future by paying off these debts, no profit for ourselves accrues from our acts of love. We have to leave our acts of love behind in the world; but they are then a

spiritual factor in the flow of world events. It is not through our acts of love but through acts of a different character that we perfect ourselves; yet the world is richer for our acts of love. Love is the creative force in the world.[3]

I experienced a fine example for a truly spiritual deed in a home for severely handicapped young people. During a meeting I noticed a lady who impressed me by her rectitude and calm presence. I assumed she was a therapist but I was told that she was the cleaning lady who had worked in this home for more than twenty years. Five boys between 12 and 17 years lived in this house, and on this particular afternoon there was an important meeting and all the staff members left to attend it, and a young trainee came to fetch the boys to take them to the workshop. However, just as she arrived, one of the boys had an epileptic fit. The other boys – each in his own way – started to make a fuss. It was total chaos, leaving the inexperienced trainee at a loss. At that moment the lady appeared on the doorstep, dust cloth in hand. As a domestic help, she was not allowed to assist the boys. She bent down and slowly started dusting the skirting boards, moving along the periphery of the room. The further she went, the calmer the boys became until total peace at returned to the room. She just knew exactly what to do without saying a word.

This example gave me an inkling of how alchemists must have worked in earlier times, how a total transformation of substances were possible because the alchemists was able to unite the spiritual with the material. Spirit becomes reality through conscious human deeds.

Overcoming stress

Many people feel overwhelmed and put themselves under pressure to keep the house in order all the time. A young mother once called me and said, 'I've been working the whole day, and now that I have just cleared the kitchen and feel totally exhausted, I cannot think of anything useful I did today.'

Together we tried to reconstruct her day. She had planned to thoroughly clean the main bathroom upstairs, but as soon as she wanted to start, she remembered that she had left the cleaning things in the laundry downstairs. There she immediately noticed that the cat's litter was very smelly and needed to be replaced. After having cleaned the container and added fresh pellets, she carried the bag and its smelly contents to the garage. Here she was confronted with piles of newspapers which had to be tied up to be collected the next day. At first she could not find the string to tie it with and looked around for ages until she finally remembered that about a week ago her son had built a funicular in the attic. When she ran up there, at least discovered the sweater her boy has been looking for all week. Once the newspaper was tied up and ready to go, it was time to cook lunch. After lunch there was a piano lesson and then a dentist appointment. And now finally, as she was brushing her teeth, she realised that the cleaning things were still in the laundry.

We are all familiar with such situations and we can understand and sympathise with it. But all the sympathising and understanding is completely useless, unless something changes. If we always have to start from scratch because chaos takes over, it can drive us to desperation. We often resolve to change things, and then all of a sudden we catch ourselves complaining, saying something about someone else, eat a third piece of pie, arrive late again, although we have ...

There is a fourth-century story handed down by hermits living in the Egyptian desert. A group of people came to a hermit and asked him, 'What is your purpose in leading your life of silence?'

He was just busy drawing some water from a deep well. He reflected for a moment and said, 'Look into the well, and tell me what you see.'

The visitors looked into the well and said, 'We don't see anything.'

After a little while he prompted them to look into the well a second time. 'What do you see now?'

They looked down into the well again and said with amazement, 'We can see ourselves.'

The hermit replied, 'Because I drew water from the well, the water was disturbed, and you could not see anything. Now that the water has become calm, you can see yourselves. This is the experience of silence.'

The story illustrates a very basic problem. Where there is no inner calm, we are unable to see ourselves and our surroundings clearly and therefore often live in disharmony.

Inner restlessness, disquiet or agitation can have many causes. It could simply be a specific incident, for instance, a disagreement with somebody in our professional life, or with someone at home. It may simply make us feel very nervous, or could cause us sleepless nights, or even palpitations or dizziness. We all know such conditions. Sometimes it's an indefinable feeling of anxiety of the unknown, a change in our lives. Such disquiet can even express itself physically.

Where does all this come from? What makes us so vulnerable? One of the main causes of inner agitation is that the different parts of our being – the self or I, the astral body, the life body and the physical body – are no longer in balance.

In his lecture, How to Cure Nervousness, Rudolf Steiner mentions two possibilities. The physical body may overwhelm the life body; this leads to a forgetfulness, absent-mindedness, uncontrolled movement (tics), carelessness, and so on. The second possibility is that the astral body overwhelms the I; we feel unsettled, anxious, and are unable to control our thoughts, and so on.

The exercises that Rudolf Steiner gave in this lecture can help us to overcome this imbalance and thereby calm the waters of our inner being. This was what the earliest Christian hermits strove for in the Egyptian desert. Here they battled with temptations and visions, with physical suffering, doubts and fears. Matthias Grünewald depicts this movingly in the Temptation of St Anthony, part of the Isenheim Altarpiece.

Prayer played a very important part in the lives of the early monks. Through prayer human beings feel united with God. Throughout the Christian centuries monks faithfully practised prayer. As the story of the hermit tells us, it was important for them to be able to look into the mirror of their soul, to look at themselves, recognise and overcome their shortcomings. Their way of relating to the world around was by retreating from it to a certain degree, either into a monastery or as a hermit into a cell.

What are the demands that we are confronted with today? We stand in the midst of all the different aspects of modern civilisation, as well as in human relationships of family and work. Finding inner calm and meaning in our lives can help us to remain healthy and balanced, and prevent over-exhaustion and burnout. 'Create moments of inner peace for yourself, and in these moments learn to distinguish the essential from the inessential.' This is one of the first steps in Rudolf Steiner's book, How to Know Higher Worlds.[4]

Observing ourselves as if from the outside helps free our I or self from dominance by the astral body. It can be difficult to be objective in our self-observation, to see ourselves as if reflected in the calm surface of water. It can initially be a help to gain the necessary distance and objectivity by contemplating events that have taken place some time ago. What is important is to practise this regularly, and to keep on trying; our continual efforts will strengthen us and help us to maintain inner calm in difficult situations.

If we manage to turn the energy we put into judgments and thoughts about the world and other people, back onto ourselves, using it for self-observation, then we can begin to overcome tensions in our relation with the world and our fellow human beings. Our strengthened self or I becomes master over the emotions and whims of our astral body. It is of course impossible for us today to spend as much time in prayer and meditation, creating a link with the divine, as the monks did in their monasteries in centuries gone by. But it is important that we try in our daily lives to create brief moments to practice inner calm. Creating a rhythm of regular inner practice in our life is soothing and healing. It can sometimes be a struggle to persevere with these exercises, but we may then find that these moments of quiet become a strength which is created through rhythm, through doing something on a regular basis. In our everyday life this strength can give us self-assurance and help us in our resolves.

Monika Kiel-Hinrichsen wrote about this practice.

> My husband is an early riser and he was happy to give me half an hour every morning that I could use as I wanted to. I used this precious time for meditation, prayer or concentration exercises, and I found it helped to strengthen my vitality.
>
> It can help the children to respect this time, by telling them that, 'Mummy is speaking to the angels.' One might even choose a particular corner of the room that is mummy's sacred place. Another mother used is to hang a picture of an angel on her door, so that her children knew not to disturb her then.[5]

Even if it is not always easy to create these quiet moments, it worth persevering. The following exercises may be of help.

Exercises for strengthening the life body

These are excellent exercises to consolidate and strengthen the life or ether body to fully penetrate and enliven the physical body.

- ❋ Consciously change your handwriting, perhaps for 10 to 15 minutes a day.
- ❋ Overcome forgetfulness by consciously putting something in a different place every day. As you put the object down, create a clear image of where you put it. If you always have to look for your glasses or keys, put them down in a different place, but clearly take in where, for instance, on the right corner of the coffee table next to the flowers.
- ❋ Strengthen your memory, by recalling events of the day in reverse order; so, start with going to bed, and end with getting up. Or recall how you laid the table by picturing removing everything in the reverse order. Review the things you have just done. For instance, after you have cleaned a room, look back to see if everything is where it is supposed to be: are the curtains hanging straight, or have you taken the chairs down from the table after mopping the floor?

Exercises for strengthening the astral body

These exercises strengthen the astral or soul body's control over the ether or life body.

- ❋ Carefully observe your actions, for instance, when you write or prepare vegetables.
- ❋ Observe and become aware of the quality of your gestures and movements, for instance when you eat or even stir your coffee. (Can I stir my coffee without making a noise banging the spoon against the side of the cup, do I put my spoon down carefully after having stirring the coffee or do I just drop it? Are my gestures when I clean flowing and harmonious, or am I all cramped up and fighting the dirt?)

❊ Try to change some of your habits. For instance, use your left hand instead of the right one if you are a right-handed person. This strengthens the control of the astral body over the ether body. For instance, try to eat with your other hand, or use your other hand to dust with or hold the vacuum cleaner.

Exercises for integrating the self

Nervousness is sometimes experienced, in that people often don't quite know how to go about doing what they really want to do. The following exercises can strengthen the will through mastering the emotions of the astral body.

❊ Practice restraint, and do not give in to every whim. Every time you refrain from following some personal whim, you strengthen your willpower. Don't drink a cup of coffee before the job is done, but enjoy it once it is accomplished.

❊ Rarely is something either right or wrong, good or bad. Usually both sides play into it. Consider the pros and contras of a situation, make a conscious decision and then keep to it. It is important that when you resolve to do something, you try everything in your power to do it. Don't just say, it will happen, but, I shall do it. For instance, do I leave something lying about, or do I pick it up immediately; do I wash the dishes, or do I let them stand around until tomorrow morning?

❊ Try to become aware of the barriers between yourself and the outside world. That entails not allowing personal opinions to influence an objective assessment of a situation.

❊ Try to avoid unnecessary opinions and judgments; less than a tenth of the criticism and opinions we form is more than enough.

6. Creating Order

The greatest happiness human beings can experience is when they are creating. Why? Because this is when they come closest to the essence of God. God is the creator, and human beings, whom he made in his image, can be creators, too. Of course, it is not a question of comparing human creations with the divine creation but of emphasising this truth, that happiness is found in the creative act, so in this sense artist express their greatest feelings of happiness. You will say, 'What about mystics and scholars?' Yes, insofar as they can also be creators, they experience the same happiness as artists.

And don't go protesting that you have known artists who were tormented and very unhappy. What I mean when I say that artists are happy is that while they are creating, in the act of creation, they live in plenitude – and 'artist' can also be taken to mean any human being in the process of creating.

Omraam Mikhaël Aïvanhov, Daily Meditations

Disorder is not chaos

For well over twenty years I have been giving lectures and workshops on the subject of cleaning and caring. One of the things that became clear is that the cleaning is not the as much of a problem as the constant disorder that many people find. Without clearing up first you cannot even start to clean.

So what is order? It is something desperately longed for by many people, and yet it seems to be so elusive.

At the very first cleaning conference I organised in 2004 at the Goetheanum, one of the lecturers said, 'Making order is a profoundly creative act, and can be put on the same level as creating works of art; perhaps it is actually be considered the archetypal artistic gesture.'[1]

When it comes to housekeeping, the concepts of disorder and chaos often get confused. In a household, order is often related to a certain regularity and clarity. We call a room orderly when everything is in its place and we can easily orientate ourselves and find our way around. However, as soon as I start working in the room, or children start playing in it, the order very soon turns into disorder. Order seems to have this special quality of effortlessly merging into disorder, yet the opposite never occurs. I have to consciously intervene to re-establish the lost order. So, disorder is simply a quality that arises whenever we do anything in an ordered space, but order can be relatively easily be reinstated.

The story of creation in the kabbala tells us that God withdrew, thus producing a void. Chaos arose within this void, and later formed the substance from which the world was then created. Chaos is a state where things have just been left to themselves without any conscious intervention (divine or human).

Disorder and order

Difficulty in making decisions is also a form of disorder when one realises how difficult it is to decide whether we are still going to use something or not. Should we actually start sorting out things, putting them where they belong, or should we leave it a bit. Some people have no difficulty in creating order, others experience great difficulty with it – they feel overwhelmed, exhausted, some even feel quite close to despair.

Working with people with difficulties in creating order, I have come to realise that they often suffer a feeling of extreme loneliness: such an extreme loneliness that they try to disguise it by being very busy with all kinds of things and accumulating things around them as if to cover up their loneliness.

Disorder usually comes about when there is too much around. Being overwhelmed is much the same thing: it is a question of too much to do. So being overwhelmed is actually a form of disorder. Disorder happens where things appear in places or situations where they do not belong. We leave something lying about; we don't finish things we started, putting them off again and again. Other things we gather, hoard and are unable to let go. Most things we leave will turn to chaos. If we ignore and leave all the things that overwhelm us, it can lead to discontent and frustration. In some cases this can even destroy family relationships.

If we are overwhelmed, we have a tendency to overwhelm others around us, for instance by saying, 'I must do this and I must do that, which absolutely needs to be done.' Says who? You say it and I say it. We are the ones who overtax ourselves with excessive expectations and the demands we set for ourselves. We are the sole reason for our lack of strength if we find ourselves once again doing something that we really didn't want to do. And we are surprised if we break things, hurt ourselves or even have accidents when we rush from one place to another, taking on task after another and never refusing to do anything asked of us.

Holding contradictory thoughts and wishes creates an inner disorder, and we should not be surprised if in these circumstances we lose our bearings. Some people complain that they don't know where they are, and feel totally lost. Why? Because they said yes to too many different things, they gave in to too many whims, collected too many different things, and now they are up to their neck in complications.

The first step away from being overwhelmed can be to begin to create order around us. It can be tremendously rewarding to start picking up things and begin to make the house tidy. Ordering can have a therapeutic effect. We become active and thereby support our own healing process, like in any therapy. If we cannot face starting with the whole house or a room, it may help to start just by emptying out our handbag, throwing away all the little things that don't really belong there. Or we can start our therapy by clearing out our wardrobe, sorting and dealing with all the unpaid bills, or whatever.

Temptation

Being overwhelmed can also be caused by a form of temptation. It may, for instance, be a hidden form of pride in believing that we are able to do more than we are actually capable of, or a feeling of being infallible or irreplaceable.

We often believe that we have unlimited capacity, unlimited time and strength. However, when the work was done, even God took a rest. On the seventh day he took a step back, and looked back on what had been done (Gen.2:2).

Without taking the time to step back and reflect on what we have done, we are in danger of rushing on to the next task, perhaps out of this hidden feeling of pride. In an extreme form this can lead to a feeling of invincible superiority. However, the other extreme is a feeling of utter helplessness and despair, a feeling that 'others' or 'the system' will take care of things. The human being continually strives to maintain a balance between these two opposing forces.

Each extreme is a temptation. Rudolf Steiner called the one tempter Lucifer who leads us away from all earthly forms, trying to make us forget responsibilities, and giving us the illusion that we are capable of anything. Too much disorder can make us want to escape from matter, weakens our will. We lose ourselves and play right into the hands of Lucifer. Losing our conscious connection to the world around us, leaves a void in which chaos grows.

The other tempter, Ahriman, tries to force us into set forms, into a kind of rigidity, and tying us down to all that is material. An obsessive attention to all around us leads to sterile order.

In each case we have lost our balance and each can eventually lead to loneliness and social isolation. Finding a happy medium is difficult to achieve, but is something we must continually strive for.

Only I know whether I am equal to my task, whether I do my work well or not. We must learn to ask ourselves why we do some things and leave others. Is it because we do not have the time just now and consciously decide to do it tomorrow, or do we just rush through the motions or even leave it completely hoping nobody will notice?

Simply despairing, saying, 'That's the way it is,' is only half the truth. The other half of this truth is what we do out of our own initiative. Ahriman tries to hinder us from doing anything out of personal freedom or initiative. Lucifer tempts us to take ever more initiatives, to start new things without finishing what has been started, and to act without consideration for the environment or social surroundings.

We need to learn to recognise these temptations, to discern which forces are leading us to do certain things, and be aware of what we decide consciously or what is simply left undone.

Strive to finish what was started

We may have experienced a friend or relative suddenly becoming very busy, trying to order everything: long postponed letters being written, bills paid, or a sudden reconciliation with a neighbour. And then our amazement changes to understanding when soon after this that friend or relative dies unexpectedly. It is as if they sensed a primordial need to order things before they set off on their ultimate journey.

I was once visiting a community for a few days working with different groups. During the first session, two gentlemen arrived telling me that they had absolutely no interest in cleaning and that I should not count on their assistance as they had no intention of participating in any on the workshops. I assured them that participation was absolutely voluntary.

On the last afternoon, a Sunday, we decided to clean the communal kitchen. We had barely started when these two gentlemen arrived, declaring that they wanted to participate in the session after all. They looked around and decided to clean the oven, as it was in desperate need to be cleaned. I took great pains to show them exactly how to go about it. They immediately tackled the job with great joy and very soon started singing merrily.

There was to be a concluding discussion at about 7 pm. So at about 6 pm I suggested that we finish our tasks, so that we would have enough time to prepare. The two gentlemen insisted that they finish the work and promised to tidy up and bring all the cleaning utensils to me when they finished. We were already sitting ready for our conversation just before 7 pm, when they brought me the utensils and told me proudly that the oven was as good as new.

Just then the resident physician who also wanted to participate in our conversation, asked us to wait a few moments as he had to organise a few things because someone had just died. We used the time to hear something about the life the deceased person from those who knew him. For many decades he had taken on the duty of cleaning the oven, and took great pride his self-appointed task. He had had an accident a few months earlier and had been bedridden since. He had often asked about the oven, and whether someone had taken on this task. He had always cleaned the oven on Sunday afternoons and always sang merrily while he worked.

It was as if he was unable to die as long as something that was important to him was not well ordered and taken care of.

The difficulty of maintaining order

THE SUMMER DRESS

With heaps of ironing surrounding me
In a hidden corner, I suddenly see
My missing summer dress with bows.
Alas! Outside just now it snows.
'Ah well,' says I, and put it where
Once summer comes, I'll find it there.
Yet as the summer came my way
I searched for it the whole damn day.
I'll search until again it snows
And then I'll find my dress with bows.[2]

Despite the enormous choice of books and media offerings about tidying and maintaining order, acquiring clutter is becoming one of the biggest epidemics of our time. Most books are usually quite effective for people who are temporarily overwhelmed, and for those who are quite active anyway and who usually have a little chaos around them simply because they are so creative. These people don't usually have any difficulty doing a big bout of clearing from time to time. But if there is a basic weakness that either is not recognised or which is denied, then these books will not be of much use, or at best give temporary relief.

Sometimes people feel threatened by a sudden clean-up. A worried husband once phoned me, saying, 'Mrs Thomas, you recommended a book to my wife last weekend about clearing. Since then she hasn't stopped clearing and throwing out things. I'm beginning to fear that I might be the next on her list.'

Of course a workshop or a book might fill someone with enthusiasm and enterprise, but I would recommend that you pause and reflect carefully on what you want to do. After a workshop a mother went home eager to immediately put into practice what she had learned. She started repairing her daughter's favourite dress that has been in her mending basket for the last few months. After having spent some time mending it, her daughter was bitterly disappointment because she had grown out of her dress.

If we have difficulties in starting to do something, it is often not the work itself that is daunting, but the mere thought of all the things that still need doing that has a crushing effect on us. Few things in life are as wearing as continual disorder and the inability to do something about it.

Another thing familiar to most of us is that, although we make a sincere effort, we often feel very alone with our feelings of inadequacy and failure. We all have certain difficulties, even though – or perhaps because – we strive so hard to overcome this problem or weakness. Personally, I am a person who is good cleaning and am creative in finding solutions to all sorts of problems, but when it comes to paperwork, I must admit I am hopeless. Often because I did not manage to finish my correspondence promptly, I was surrounded by paper and had to spend a lot of time looking for things I needed. This sometimes led to despair because I really wanted to keep my paperwork tidy. In the end I found a solution by employing someone to come to my house for a few hours every week. She not only helps with my correspondence, but also does the filing, organises and books all my trips, agrees terms with my clients, writes the invoices, and so on. Once I recognised my weakness, I was able to delegate it to a capable person. This solution brought relief, not only to me, but to the whole family, by greatly reducing my stress. But it was not an easy decision for someone convinced of her own efficiency and being able to do everything just right. Yet I have not regretted it for a moment and have decided to tackle that particular personal weakness later.

Then there are some people who always seem to have perfect order, but have the tendency to overwhelm those around them with very high standards and demands. Nobody feels at ease if the table is wiped, the cloth smoothed, the furniture adjusted after every use. Order should serve – not rule our lives.

As I mentioned before, it helps if we consider our home like an organism. Something as self-evident and natural as the process of eating, digesting and eliminating, needs to be considered in our household. Obviously the digestive process in a house takes a little longer than in a human being, but if nothing is ever eliminated from a house, not only the house but also the members of the household risk suffering severe indigestion or constipation.

Caring and creating order has an emanation that radiates beyond the immediate area. This can be an antidote to disorder and decay. Have you ever tried to create such an antidote by picking up rubbish from some public area?

We once stopped at busy highway rest area. The bins were running over, and garbage was lying on the ground around them. We cleared up everything around the bin closest to us, and observed what happened next. Where there were still things lying on the ground, people did not hesitate to drop rubbish, yet our area remained orderly, and people carefully deposited the rubbish in the bin. As an experiment we put one piece of paper on the ground next to our bin, and within moments it had company.

We can observe a similar tendency in our own home. When my children were quite young, we had installed hooks for their satchels in our hallway. Every day they would dutifully hang up their satchels on the hooks before taking off their coats. Once, just as I came into the house with my shopping, the telephone rang. I left the two shopping bags in the hallway and rushed to answer the phone. At that moment my children came home, and their satchels landed on the floor next to the shopping bags.

We can see from these examples that simple, small steps can have a wider effect. We can choose some corner of our house – a little table or even a sill – and concentrate on always keeping this area orderly, well cared for and beautiful. The light and strength from this area will radiate into the whole home.

In an interview Erich Fromm, a German-American psychologist, said, 'Vitality itself is the result of vision. If there is no longer a vision of something great, beautiful or important, then our vitality and stamina diminish.'[3]

Where does disorder start?

Disorder always starts with a decision, however trivial. Do I put the newspaper I have just read in the recycling bin, or do I leave it where it is? Do I close the door or the drawers in the kitchen cabinet after having fetched something, or do they remain open, sometimes just a little bit? Do I put things back into their right place when I pick them up, or do I just leave them where I've used them? Disorder is often a direct consequence of hurry or impatience, and not taking the time for that extra step.

Some people have such high standards for certain tasks that they obsessively repeat them again and again, and never get on with the next thing. The bathroom might be spotless and shining like a new penny while other things are in desperate need of attention. Or they lose themselves in unnoticed details while the rest of the room still looks chaotic. Other people are sentimental, and feel they have two keep every single drawing of each of their children, or every little pine cone or pebble they brought in from playing outside. Most of us are, of course, somewhere between these two extremes.

It is important to recognise the real reason behind our problem, but we also have to recognise its outer manifestation. What should we try to resolve first: the inner or the outer problem? Personally, I believe we should tackle both at the same time. Deal with the outer disorder in small, careful steps, and at the same time make a conscious inner decision to make a regular effort to overcome our habits.

It helps to set small, manageable daily targets rather than trying to turn the whole house upside down in one go. It can simply be clearing out one drawer every day. Perseverance is important, for breaking off and leaving things for some days weakens our resolve, making it counts, because taking too many breaks could weaken the will to such an extent that it will only become more and more difficult to start again. We have to learn to observe ourselves carefully during this process, to recognise the signs before we fall back into old habits. Most importantly, we must realise that we ourselves are the only one who can make the decision to do this. No matter how good the advice or suggestions are that we receive, what we finally do, depends solely on ourselves and our own efforts. It is a decision that has to arise out of our own free will without any coercion or outside pressure. In that way we retain or even enhance our dignity. Once we have taken this step it may help us to distinguish the essential from the inessential, to set priorities, and – most importantly – to regain confidence in our own ability.

The two most important steps are first, from having to do something to wanting to do it, and secondly, from wanting to do something to actually doing it.

If we genuinely want to make a change, but realise that we are simply unable to do so, then we must recognise this as a weakness that we might tackle later, and in the meantime get someone to help.

Where do I start?

Before we start it is important to set a goal, something that we can aim at. One such a goal could of course be to have a perfectly ordered house. But that is a tall order, and not every single corner has to be done at the same time. In order not to be overwhelmed, we need to focus on the essentials, and set priorities.

Before we start cleaning, decide which room needs our attention most. Once we have decided on what we are going to do first, it helps to prepare everything we need for the task the evening before. (Our will is activated quite differently if, having decided on something, we then sleep on it.) When we are ready to start, we should pause for a moment in the doorway of that room and ask, 'What is the first thing I should do?' It is most probably the thing that we have avoided doing for a long time. Once we have made up our mind, we should start with doing just that, and not get sidetracked into half a dozen inessential tasks.

Once the first task is completed, return to the threshold and look at the room again. Did it make a difference? What should be next on our list? Be persistent and keep setting priorities, each time asking what is essential. If you start feeling muddled, sit down and think, 'What next?' Practice economy of actions, and try not to handle anything more than once (for instance, try not to move something to a temporary place before finally sorting it out).

Once you get started, overcoming the initial 'blockage', you will probably feel a surge of energy and confidence, and will simply want to continue. Many people have told me that once this hurdle was crossed, they could feel their strength returning. So it is important not to get lost in details at this stage, but to continue taking small steps towards the goal. If we decide to do at least twenty things on the first day, there is a far greater likelihood that the day will end with a feeling of discontent, frustration and failure.

Developing willpower

If we plan to do too many things, it becomes impossible to commit to them all. We will be trying to think of all things at the same time. While ironing we are already think about the shopping list. At some point we may become so restless that we may leave the ironing to go shopping. While shopping, we're busy thinking about the seedlings we want to plant when I get home. Then while we're in the garden we remember that we wanted to bake a cake, and then going inside we see that we left the iron on ...

Nothing ever gets properly finished, because we are continually chasing the next task that pops into our head, leaving a trail of uncompleted actions. We are unable to savour the present moment and enjoy the task at hand. It can sap our energy if we are confronted with unfinished business at every turn. The cause of all these unfinished things is a strange a form of greed. We want to do more than we need to or can manage. The resulting frustration and stress may even lead to burnout or a breakdown.

To have a strong will does not mean that we have to constantly be active, rushing about doing a hundred and ten things. Strong willpower shows itself more clearly if we assume responsibility for everything we take on. That includes the things we actually manage to do as well as those we leave undone. Taking on this responsibility develops self-confidence, strengthens us and gives us the energy for our next task.

It is not the work we have done which tires is as much as the mountain of things still to do. The chaos of all the things we intend to do robs us of our strength and even of our dignity. However, each action we have done, however small and insignificant, give us strength and fills us with a sense of achievement and self-esteem. Every conscious deed frees us and helps to harmonise our environment.

Self help and getting help

Becoming aware of our habits is the first step to deciding to change them. I once helped an elderly lady to clear her kitchen. In one of the cupboards there were hundreds of empty sugar bags that she had been collecting for years. When I asked her what they were for, she answered, 'They're perfect for the children's sandwiches.' I gently pointed out that by now her children were probably making sandwiches for their own children. For a moment she looked at me quite dumbfounded and then she burst out laughing.

Sometimes people manage to clear up the disorder themselves, simply because they discovered a very good reason to start doing it. I was once asked to help two people during their mother's stay in hospital. Ever since her daughter and son left home she began to hoard things, filling up one room after another. Before then she had always been a tidy person. The son and daughter had resolved to use their mother's absence and at least free the bathroom from the newspapers which filled it to the top. When their mother returned she was so shocked that she threatened suicide if her children would ever do such a thing again. Her daughter had two young girls who loved their grandmother dearly. She would often visit her daughter and granddaughters, but they were unable to visit her because there was no room in the house.

I suggested that the siblings should find a good reason to 'need' to bring the girls to their grandmother. The daughter planned a trip with her husband, and invited friends to stay in her house while they were away, making it impossible for the grandmother to take care of the girls in the family home. This then led to the grandmother out of herself asking her children to help clear her cluttered house.

If our standards are too high, we may frighten people off, because we give them the feeling that whatever they do, it is not good enough. A mother once told me that she had a very strong need for order, and her children were only allowed to play with one thing at a time, and no new game was to be brought out unless the old playthings had been tidied away. One day, her four-year-old boy was sitting on the stairs rather morosely, instead of playing. When she asked him why he was not playing, he replied, 'Oh, after I play I always have to tidy up everything.' She realised then that her standards had spoilt her son's joy in playing.

Another danger is if our desire for order is greater than what we actually manage in practice. Our demands of others seem even more unjustified, because we appear to be hypocritical. It is even worse if we are unaware of the fact that we have not yet acquired the qualities to which we aspire. Then we lose all credibility. Through our own actions we have to set a good example, and if we request something it must not become a demand.

Marshall Rosenberg told the story of a mother asking a friend (who was also a family therapist) for advice because her three young sons would not help with household chores.[4] She was of the opinion that everyone should do something, even if they did not like doing it. After all, she did things she hated doing. When asked what she did not like doing, she replied, 'I hate cooking, but have to prepare meals several times a day.' The therapist suggested that the boys should take over the cooking while the mother should take care of the rest of the household. A few weeks later, the therapist met one of the sons and asked how things were going at home. He replied, 'Since we took on the cooking, we've been having happy mealtimes without discord It was never like that before.'

Khalil Gibran in *The Prophet* said following:

> And if you cannot work with love but only with distaste, it is
> better that you should leave your work and sit at the gate of
> the temple and take alms from those who work with joy. For
> if you bake bread with indifference, you bake bitter bread that
> feeds but half man's hunger. And if you grudge the crushing
> of the grapes, your grudge distils a poison in the wine.

Real, living order, affects people in a positive way.

A farmer who quite often wrote articles, told me during a seminar that he now understood why it was often so hard for him to write. He did not allow anyone else to tidy up his office, and would always do it himself – but unfortunately not often enough. He had noticed that after he had clean up his office he could always write well, but he had never really thought about the connection. Now he would try to tidy and clean his office regularly, saving a lot of time, as he would be able to sit down and write without having to clean up first.

When we look at the effect of order, we can see that we are rewarded a hundredfold. The inner strength we invest to create order connects us to a higher, cosmic order which lights up our soul giving us a wonderful feeling of harmony.

Dust and neglect

'Charity begins at home.' Often people look for activities outside the home – even charitable work – just to be able to escape their own four walls. Young mothers who attend my workshops often list all the many things they do as volunteers – wonderful, selfless activities. With that they justify their inability to do the necessary tasks at home. One mother even told me, 'I buy beautiful bouquets of flowers every week so that my children only notice the flowers and not the mess.' I asked her why she did not get a cleaner to help. She immediately answered that it would be far too expensive. When we calculated the cost of the flowers, we found that she could afford help for at least three hours a week.

In order to clean anything, we must first tidy up and restore order. The more things we have, the harder it is to establish and maintain order. Once the clutter gets completely out of hand, the home becomes neglected or even squalid. While order and care have a radiant quality, neglect is something insidious. It begins in the corners and places that we disregard; it creeps from window sills that have become a veritable graveyard of dead insects among the pine cones, crystals and plants; it invades the curtains where the spiders have taken up residence, and marches under the beds where dust balls chase each other between the many items stuffed there.

A small table, decorated according to the season, can beautify our home, but as soon as dust or even dead flies collect there, our children lose interest. As soon as we clear the tablecloth and add fresh flowers, they take pleasure in it again.

If we do not manage to cultivate and care for our surroundings, it will begin to affect us. Internal or external care declines, often both. We may look well groomed, but may not be sleeping as well, or we may be plagued by anxiety.

If we observe life we can see that there is always growth and decay, but nothing remains unchanged. Something must wither and die for a fresh start to be possible. Development is not possible without change. The old passes away, allowing something new to arise. Although many people experience change as a misfortune, it is necessary so. Sometimes it is not until many years later that we realise the benefit certain changes brought us.

People who think they do not need to change stagnate. Some people are terrified of the empty space that a change such as retirement or separation may bring. They live in fear and uncertainty of a mindless void, for they have not learned to be content in their own company. It is useless to try to fill such a spiritual, emotional void with material things. Unless we have really experienced this void, we cannot create a new life, find new content, and thus embark on a process of transformation.

It is important to strive to live in the way we really wish to live. If we feel, 'I cannot stand this for another three years,' we should immediately seek to reorganise and transform our life. If we are simply resigned to an attitude of 'What will be, will be,' we are at risk of being overwhelmed. However, if we resolve to change something and then actually do it, we are taking a step in the right direction.

Clearing out strengthens the ability to let go and the trust that we will have what we need. It may be helpful to look at the things that surround us, and form a picture of which things disturb us, or perhaps even discover which things are lacking.

There are also non-material 'things'. Things we remember, things we have to do, things which trouble us or give us joy. Many enrich our lives, others exhaust us, draining our strength and energy. We are connected with all these things. It can be a new and exciting challenge to find a new relationship to such things, and it may even help us create order and allow something new in our life.

7. Our Relation to the Objects Around Us

Bidding farewell

Stages

As every flower fades and as all youth
Departs, so life at every stage,
So every virtue, so our grasp of truth,
Blooms in its day and may not last forever.
Since life may summon us at every age
Be ready, heart, for parting, new endeavor,
Be ready bravely and without remorse
To find new light that old ties cannot give.
In all beginnings dwells a magic force
For guarding us and helping us to live.
Serenely let us move to distant places
And let no sentiments of home detain us.
The Cosmic Spirit seeks not to restrain us
But lifts us stage by stage to wider spaces.
If we accept a home of our own making,
Familiar habit makes for indolence.
We must prepare for parting and leave-taking
Or else remain the slaves of permanence.
Even the hour of our death may send
Us speeding on to fresh and newer spaces,

And life may summon us to newer races.
So be it, heart: bid farewell without end.[1]

The final line of the poem 'Stages' by Hermann Hesse (1877–1962) is perhaps applicable not only to human beings but also to objects. The phrase 'bid farewell' is not only a taking leave of someone or something, it expresses a hope and a wish for the other to keep in good health, to 'fare well'.

We are surrounded by a multitude of objects, bought, collected, then stored away, and ultimately thoughtlessly thrown away. Some people are unable to throw things away although the often feel oppressed by all the objects they have accumulated over the years. We might even wonder whether the objects 'suffer' from neglect or thoughtless disposal, as is told in some fairy tales.

If we develop a sense of devotion to and a healthy respect for all material things, we will acquire a sense of which things make us feel comfortable and at ease, and which objects affect our environment in a negative way.

We receive gifts, and although we really do not like them, keep them because we do not want to hurt the people who gave them to us. This may be kind, but are we being kind to ourselves? Do we not 'hurt' ourselves if we are surrounded by things that bring us no joy, or perhaps even fill us with resentment?

It is sometimes difficult to decide how we can get dispose of a gift which occupies a place of honour, although we cannot stand it. Fortunately, we sometimes get help in unexpected ways.

A participant of one of my seminars went home, determined to get rid of such a gift, a lamp that had occupied a special place for years in her living room. She was annoyed by it almost daily, but could not summon the courage to discard it. The next morning at the seminar, she told us, 'All the way home I was strengthening my resolve to finally dispose of this lamp, even if it might disturb the family peace for a while. No sooner had I arrived at the front door, than my daughter came out, telling me how the cat had pushed grandmother's lamp off the cabinet and that it had shattered into a thousand pieces.'

Once we firmly resolve to do something, sometimes nature comes to our aid. As William Hutchinson Murray so aptly says, 'the moment one definitely commits oneself, then Providence moves too. All sorts of things occur to help one that would never otherwise have occurred.'[2]

Once a newlywed couple came to a seminar to learn more about housekeeping. They had met each other when they were both forty-two, and for both it was their first relationship. Seeing the two together, one immediately sensed a strong and harmonious bond. About half a year later, the lady called me in despair, 'Linda, my marriage is falling apart.'

I told her that I could not believe it, but she replied, 'It has to be something in our house. As soon as we enter the house, we somehow stop talking to each other. When we go shopping, go out to eat, or go for a walk, we are as happy as ever. But the moment we open the door to our apartment, it's like ice between us.'

She mentioned that this had been going on for ten days, but she could not think of any changes which had taken place in that time. I suggested she should imagine herself standing on the threshold, carefully observing to see if anything was different. Suddenly she remembered a piano and explained that her mother had moved into a nursing home ten days ago, and that she had to have the piano. The words 'had to' immediately caught my attention, so I asked her what the piano meant to her.

'I hate the piano!' she exploded. 'My mother always wanted me to be a pianist, and I had to spend hours practising every day. I cannot stand it.'

The solution was obvious. I suggested that she should give away the piano and visit her mother so often that she would not feel a need to visit her daughter at home. Then she would probably never find out that the piano had found a worthier home. But it was important to find the right home for the piano, knowing that it was not to blame for the hours she had to spend practising. The piano was given to a music school that was very grateful for the gift. The tension caused by the unpleasant memories arising at the sight of the hated piano was gone, and the couple was as happy as ever.

It is often the case that one small thing can disturb the atmosphere in a room. It can sometimes be a single letter in a drawer. So if we sense an inexplicable unease when we enter a room, we can try and track down the hated piano.

In a village community for adults with special needs, I was told about a house which had a particularly negative energy. Almost everyone who moved into this house had difficulties after a time. Children became sick, residents began to bicker, or arguments flared between spouses. This went on for some years, and it became so bad that the house remained empty most of the time. Recently a new family had come to this community, and because of lack of space they were obliged to use the house again. Shortly after the new residents had moved in, the house was flooded and all the carpets had to be removed. They were surprised to discover a trapdoor under the carpet in the dining room. The door led to a cellar that nobody in the village seemed to know about. When the trapdoor was opened it was like opening Pandora's box: a strong smell of mould and rot filled the air, most of the things stored down there were mouldy or rotten. They decided to burn everything. The room was ventilated for several days, freshly painted and put back into use. From that day on, there was peace in the house.

These are examples of unpopular and unappreciated things. It is possible that even certain beloved things can influence a room negatively. A client once asked me to look at her apartment because she always felt a strange tension in a particular place. I went through the apartment and after taking only two steps into the bedroom, I stopped. 'Yes, it's right there,' she said.

I looked at the room very closely to try to find a possible reason for the tension I also felt very clearly. The place where I had stopped was in a line connecting the corners of an escritoire and a dresser facing each other diagonally across the room.

'It is caused by these two pieces of furniture,' I said. The lady had difficulty believing me, because she particularly loved these two pieces which were obviously very well cared for and also used frequently. She had also inherited the escritoire from her mother and the chest of drawers from her mother's sister who was also her godmother.

I asked a few more questions and discovered that these pieces of furniture had caused a rift between the two sisters when their mother died. Unfortunately, one of the sisters died before they could be reconciled. We found an immediate solution by moving the desk into a different room.

It is important to be aware of the things that surround us in our daily lives. Certain things may distress us while others are a constant source of joy. Whether we are aware of it or not, there is a relationship between human beings and the inanimate objects surrounding us.

Favourite objects

Of course, there are many examples to prove how beneficially very well loved and cared for objects can influence us. Shortly after I started my company, an elderly lady asked me if I could help her clean her house every two weeks. On my first visit, I almost lost courage. The first thing I noticed, were well over a hundred small porcelain figurines covering almost every free surface in the living room. They were tiny figures of people, animals, dwarves, even trees, mushrooms, a small house, and suchlike. This is going to be a very time-consuming task, I thought to myself. She showed me the whole house and finally, back in the living room, she very lovingly pointed to the figures and said, 'Please don't touch the little ones, Linda, but do take special care of the spaces between the groups of figurines.' I realised that the lady was intimately connected to each one of these little characters; they were very much part of her daily life. Each small group represented a fairy tale or a specific image.

Such objects are alive, imbued with love, and give strength and joy to their owner. I soon realised that I was looking forward to visiting her house, just to discover the new groupings and images that would be there to greet me.

The value of interest

After reading the following passage by Rudolf Steiner, a totally new dimension opened up for me regarding my dealing with things.

The sentient soul is what enables the human being to experience the world of objects, to come into a relationship with the objects rather than passing them by unknowingly ... What is it that enables us to have a relationship with our surroundings? It is what we may call our interest in things. This word 'interest' expresses something that in a moral sense is extremely significant. It is much more important to bear in mind the moral significance of interest than to devote oneself to a multitude of moral axioms, which may be beautiful or perhaps also trivial and sanctimonious. Our moral impulses are in fact never guided better than when we take proper interest in objects or beings. Please think about this. Because we spoke in yesterday's lecture of the deeper meaning of love, I will not be misunderstood when I say that even the usual, oft-repeated saying of 'love, love, and love again,' cannot replace the moral impulses that lies behind the little word 'interest'.

... When we extend our interests, when we find opportunity to enter with understanding into the objects and beings of the world, our inner forces are called forth. If we take an interest in a person, our compassion is called forth in an appropriate manner. (...). Progress is not made by the mere preaching of universal love, but by the extension of our interest further and further, so that we increasingly come to be interested in and to understand people with widely different temperaments and personalities, with widely different racial and national characteristics, with widely different religious and philosophical views. Right understanding, right interest, calls forth from the soul the right moral conduct.[3]

This passage helped me to understand why people who do not engage with their environment and its objects often suffer because of their surroundings. Repeated failure in attempting to tidy and create order can lead to depression. To counteract depression it is helpful to develop a lively and genuine interest for what surrounds us. The inner flexibility that arises from such an interest can stimulate us to begin to improve conditions, and can give us the necessary constancy and perseverance.

But how can housework become a creative activity? In *The Poetics of Space*, Gaston Bachelard describes it most beautifully.

> Objects that are cherished in this way really are born of
> an intimate light, and they attain to a higher degree of
> reality than indifferent objects, or those that are defined by
> geometric reality. For they produce a new reality of being,
> and they take their place not only in an order but in a
> community of order. From one object in a room to another,
> housewifely care weaves the ties that unite a very ancient
> past to the new epoch. The housewife awakens furniture
> that was asleep.[4]

What a lovely thought, that I am able to create a new object by lovingly caring for it! Our soul accompanies this process, our touch bestows warmth. Thus we may imbue the thing that we hold in our hands with a touch of spirit. Something human is transferred to the object and enters it; and, in return, it makes a positive and beneficial impact on the human being. Rudolf Steiner expressed this in a verse:

> Seek the truly practical material life, but seek it in
>   such a way
> That it does not numb you to the spirit that works
>   with in it.
> Seek the spirit, but not out of spiritual lust or
>   spiritual egoism;
> But seek it rather because you want to apply it
>   selflessly In the practical life of the material world.

> Turn to the ancient principle:
> 'Spirit is never without matter,
> Matter never without spirit.'
> And say to yourself,
> We will do everything material in light of the spirit,

And we will seek the light of the spirit in such a way
That it enkindles warmth in us for our practical deeds.

Spirit that is guided by us into matter,
Matter that is transformed by us to reveal the spirit,
Whereby matter presses out of the spirit;
Matter, which receives from us revealed spirit,
Spirit, which is pressed by us towards matter,
These create the living existence
That can lead humanity to real progress
To the kind of progress that can only be yearned for
By the highest strivings in the deepest regions of the
   souls of our time.

What we give to objects

Observing an old servant at work, the French poet Henri Bosco (1888–
1976) wrote:

> The soft wax entered into the polished substance under the
> pressure of hands and the effective warmth of a woolen cloth.
> Slowly the tray took on a dull luster. It was as though the
> radiance induced by magnetic rubbing emanated from the
> hundred-year-old sapwood, from the very heart of the dead
> tree, and spread gradually, in the form of light, over the tray.
> The old fingers possessed of every virtue, the broad palm,
> drew from the solid block with its inanimate fibers, the latent
> powers of life itself. This was creation of an object, a real act
> of faith, taking place before my enchanted eyes.

Bosco also speaks about the integration of awareness into the humblest of occupations when he describes the work of his old faithful servant, Sidoine.

> This vocation for happiness, so far from prejudicing her
> practical life, nurtured its action. When she washed a sheet

or a tablecloth, when she polished a brass candlestick, little movements of joy mounted from the depths of her heart, enlivening her household tasks. She did not wait to finish these tasks before withdrawing into herself, where she could contemplate to her heart's content the supernatural images that dwelt there. Indeed, figures from this land appeared to her familiarly, however commonplace to work she was doing, and without in the least of seeming to dream, she washed, dusted and swept in the company of angels.

When we earnestly perceive things or events in the world, we connect with their essence. Through connecting with something, we share with it some of our essence. The world responds to the human being and shares its own nature with us. Communication takes place and objects and spaces begin to tell us something. Thus we bestow the strength of our self, the warmth of our soul, as well as our life force directly to the space or object in our care. We give of ourselves, and a part of us lives in that object or space. Omraam Mikhaël Aïvanhov spoke of the transformation of objects.

Should a distinction be made between sacred and profane objects? You live in a house or an apartment. In this flat or this house, there are several rooms in which you have placed all sorts of objects. The reason you have put them there is that they are either useful to you or you love them, which puts you in daily contact with them. So why not think of consecrating these objects. If you dedicate them to the good and to the light, they will have a beneficial effect on you and your family. And once they are made sacred, you should treat them with respect, with caution, because the way you treat them will reflect back on you. Even if this idea is not familiar to you, try to understand that by means of these considerations, you can transform the objects surrounding you into sacred objects, which are connected to heaven, and that the beneficial energy that flows through them, is also be of benefit to you.[7]

Objects have their dignity and their rightful place, on a small or large scale. Dieter Zimmermann, an artist who creates works of art from bits and pieces of everyday objects discarded by our affluent society, writes on his website that he aims, 'To elevate the rejected to a new dignity.'[8]

Compulsive hoarding

If we are unable to let go of any objects, there is a danger of compulsive hoarding, sometimes also called messie syndrome. The term messie syndrome was coined by Sandra Felton, an American teacher who was incapable of keeping any kind of order. During the 1980s she described her difficulties to change her behaviour and get control over her life again.[9] Today she has written many bestselling books that started an avalanche of self-help manuals for creating order. She calls someone suffering from this affliction a 'messie', and estimates that there are around 33 million messies in the United States (which is 12 percent of the population). It is difficult to ascertain precise figures, because most messies do not admit to being sufferers.

She defines a messie as a person whose degree of domestic order does not correspond to the norm generally accepted by society, and whose habits could cause serious problems in their life and in human relationships. A true messie has lost all control over their situation and the resulting disorder negatively affects themselves and their loved ones. They are continually under pressure, and this causes extreme stress that can manifest physically in backaches, headaches, digestive or breathing disorders.

To be able to understand and help people in this situation, it is important to look for the causes which can be diverse. Not every person who has suffered a loss ends up being a messie, but every messie I have met has suffered a lost at some point in their lives. If the ensuing void is not filled, it can grow, becoming a gaping abyss that demands to be filled. Many people do not know how to fill the emotional void, and start filling up their home with more and more stuff until chaos takes over.

Other causes are often found in deficiencies of their early development, usually in the first three years of childhood.

⁂ If the basic needs of a child were not properly met and they suffered deprivation, it can affect their self-esteem later in life. If, for instance, they suffered from hours of hunger or thirst, it can later evoke a feeling that they are unworthy of having a well cared for, orderly home or even personal appearance.

⁂ Through a prolonged or permanent separation from their mother or carer, children can experience emotional abandonment. The lack of bonding can cause a lifetime of existential fears. They feel unable to meet life's demands lack self-confidence. They often feel threatened by their surroundings because they experience other people as opponents rather than partners. Rather than accepting help from others, they rely on their relationships with material things, because physical objects will not abandon them. Insecurity and fear of relating to other people can trigger feelings of futility and emptiness.

⁂ If a child is hindered in developing autonomy, the development of their will is also weakened. This can impair their decision-making in later years.

⁂ If people do not allow sufficient time to grieve after a painful experience, such as loss of a job, divorce or bereavement, loneliness and inner confusion, can then be compensated by external disorder.

⁂ Separation or bereavement can cause some people to lose their will to live and their purpose in life. Feelings of worthlessness and futility reinforce inner chaos which will express itself in chaotic surroundings.

Not every disorderly person is a messie

Not every person who is surrounded by disorder or chaos is necessarily a messie. However, some disorganised people hide behind this label 'messie', simply because it sounds better than disorganised or slovenly. From the media we might have the impression that messies are found only in the lower social classes. But these people are from all walks of life. Their schedules are over-full, often compensating for an inability to organise their time. Scientists, poets, writers, philosophers and artists may live with this suffering. And while their achievements may inspire the world at large, many yearn to enjoy one day of peace in ordered surroundings. How does it happen that some people we admire suffer from disorder, hoarding or neglect?

Many artists may believe that because of their talent they don't have to live according to the rules and discipline of society. Others may feel that the imbalance in their lives and the anguish they suffer nurture their talents, and therefore feel justified. Undeniably great philosophical or artistic works are born from intense suffering which their creators have overcome through extreme effort. However, to really overcome these problems, self-knowledge and striving is necessary, otherwise they will simply cause suffering and anxiety, degenerating into chaos.

A phrase I have often heard is, 'Idiots need order, but a genius rules over chaos.' But among the many chaotic people I have met, genius was sadly lacking.

There are circumstances which can cause a person to be temporarily overwhelmed and unable to create order, such as a long illness, the birth of a child or depression. If disorder is caused by something like that, the people concerned will often welcome help, whereas true messies find it more difficult to accept help, because they are unaware or do not admit that they have a problem.

If the cause of disorder is due to circumstances and people ask for help, it is a good start to ask them what disturbs them most. By starting with there, it is often possible to eliminate the cause of the disorder.

A client once asked me to help ordering her apartment, because she was unable to sort the mess out by herself. She had always been an orderly person, yet within a few months, chaos seemed to have taken over. She said, her bedroom needed urgent clearing, as she was hardly able to move around in it. Personally I didn't find it that bad, but the desk in her bedroom was piled so high with stuff that things had fallen down and were covering most of the floor around it. I took a close look at the room and then asked her, 'What are you hiding at the bottom of this desk? What is all this covering up?'

She was totally shaken, looked at me furiously, and then started crying. It turned out that there was a letter from her sister with whom she was in a serious dispute concerning the inheritance from their parents. She experienced the situation is extremely painful, and did not have the courage to answer her sister's letter. It took quite a bit of time and effort to retrieve this letter from beneath the masses of paper. Once we found it, I suggested she should reply immediately. At first she could hardly breathe, she paced the room like a caged animal, sweating profusely. It took her more than half an hour to calm down sufficiently to do it. Then she quickly addressed the envelope and immediately took it to the post. When she came home, she was a transformed person. Her whole face was relaxed and there was a bounce in her step. She now really wanted to start working and within a few hours we had managed to clear up and thoroughly clean the whole bedroom. It was clear that this was not a real case of messie syndrome.

Finding solutions

Experience shows self help books very rarely help in cases of real compulsive hoarding, or at best just temporarily. Even large scale clearing out by others is mostly pointless. The new gaping void needs to be filled again, because no inner change towards the situation has taken place. The symptom has been treated, not the cause.

The brother of a colleague of mine had attended a workshop, and immediately asked her to help him clean up. She was quite happy and willing to do so, and they did a great job. However, the next day he had to be admitted to a hospital because of acute psychosis. It was as if he had received an overdose of medication.

I had the opportunity for fourteen months to accompany a self-help group for messies with Veronika Schröter, an psychotherapy practitioner and compulsive hoarding specialist in Freiburg, Germany. It was very clear to me that hoarders need expert assistance tailored to their specific symptoms. She works with clients as well as their partners and family members in therapeutic seminars, group and individual sessions. She has launched a scientific study with the University of Freiburg into the symptoms and their causes.

I wish to mention same aspects of Veronika Schröter's accounts and findings.[10]

Often the messie phenomenon has the function of protecting the victims from the repetition of past violations. By looking at their own life story, they are often able to track down the personal causes of their problems, and then learn to lovingly accept themselves with their story. They rediscover their own dignity and self-esteem. Out of their own initiative they are then able to tackle the mess step by step. Once compulsive hoarding is considered as a mental disorder, an appropriate therapy has a chance of succeeding. The goal is to give the possibility of moving freely between a normal, 'healthy' disorder and self-determined order, where before they were not in a position of making any kind of choice at all.

The clients will benefit from the best all-round support if all professional groups involved work together to accompany the therapeutic process. This enables them to make fundamental and sustainable changes.

Implications for professionals and family members

Professionals in the health and care of the elderly, as well as social workers and therapist, often feel just as helpless as family members when dealing with messies. Neither benevolent prompting nor confrontation or threats bring any fundamental changes, but may cause resistance. The conflict between feeling powerless and the sincere desire to help is a major challenge for professionals and family. The need to act is often triggered by the hygienic conditions, the concern for the well-being of vulnerable children in the home, or legitimate complaints of landlords or neighbours.

To actively intervene either forcing such people to clean up or having it done by a third party, leave them without any personal responsibility. This strengthens their feeling of incompetence, resulting in resignation and lack of self-confidence. Before long the old state will reappear.

The therapeutic process can take place in individual counselling or in a support group such as a seminars or workshops. Many participants experience the exchange with other sufferers to be very helpful. Their isolation is broken and they receive valuable input and support for their own development. Partners and family members may also be involved in the process.

Home visits are a helpful supporting measure, as the personal problem areas can be experienced, which makes it easier to develop appropriate therapeutic strategies.

Getting help at home

As previously, we can ask what should be tackled first, the inner or the outer problem? Again, I recommend both at the same time. One of my clients had been in therapy for over twelve years, and although she recognised the root of her problem, the condition in her home had slowly grown worse. Her will was not activated.

The exterior can be transformed in small well-considered steps – preferably with an experienced outside person. It is usually better not to work with family members or someone close because it exposes a vulnerable side. Interestingly, when I visit clients, I find that they often plan far too much for our session. This is part of the decision-making problem, as well as showing they have no idea how much time is needed. They proudly show me ambitious plans for their cleanup, often so extensive and complicated that I understand immediately why they have never managed. At the beginning, we have to agree on the pace. It is important not to overdo it; cleaning up a typical messie household needs a lot of patience – it is a marathon, not a sprint.

With one of my clients, the first thing we planned was to find all the documents needed for the long-overdue tax return. But before we started, I suggested cleaning up a little table in the living room. We cleared away everything that did not belong there, cleaned and decorated it. I insisted that it should remain that way, and that it would be the first thing I'd check on my return visits. Only then did we start looking for the necessary documents.

During this process we organised a practical, simple filing system, so that all documents could be filed immediately when I arrived on future visits. It is impossible to expect that after just one visit, she would be able to do it of herself. As a longer-term goal, she wanted to clean up the apartment so that she would be able to invite guests to her birthday in nine months' time. She had not done this in decades.

We started with the kitchen, followed by the hallway and then the balcony. Every time we first spent time clearing away the mountains of new papers, sorting them and filing important documents. A week before her birthday we had actually managed to clean up all that we had intended. and she could invite guests. The whole process had required just over a hundred hours of input from me.

It is essential to decide where to start and then consistently work towards the goal. There should be no external pressure to do something to satisfy the expectations of others. Such people need to make the decision themselves out of their own sincere need, with their own willpower. They will then be acting in total freedom and personally assuming responsibly for their actions.

Organising your own day

A structured, well-organised day strengthens us and fills us with energy – even if initially it requires a lot of effort and courage to plan everything sensibly. But it is worth it, because structure and rhythm add to our sense of security and support us in our endeavours. Ask someone you trust to help plan your appointments, trying to stick to a regular rhythm; for instance, yoga on Tuesdays at 10, shopping on Thursdays at 2, laundry on Fridays at 8, and so on. Plan your day around recurring events and respecting your personal preferences. This will help keep to the rhythm. The better you plan your day, the more time and energy you'll have to actually do what was planned, rather than losing time in trying to make decisions about what to do. Make sure you make plan at least ten minutes a day, to do some clearing and ordering.

Do not set your standards too high; relapses are part of the learning process giving the possibility of starting afresh. The should not be seen as failure. Avoid situations that will discourage and frustrate you.

Don't neglect your personal needs: enjoy a concert, go to the cinema, spend time with friends, or take a walk to help clear your head. You have to really set your mind to regaining your health.

To clear up means to create space. But in order to create space, you first have to create distance. A healthy distance is the first step of clearing up. A colleague of mine, Hans-Christian Zehnter, once described creating order as follows.

If we are too close to an object we neither see its form nor can we sense something of the mood or atmosphere it brings. Form, mood, atmosphere are supersensory aspects of reality; and by being too close to an object we cannot take them in. To experience their presence we need some distance. We have to include these qualities when working in a space, when cleaning or creating order. We can then transform something that causes distress, into something filled with order, beauty and lustre, all the qualities contained in the Greek word 'cosmos'.

Questions and Answers

What do you consider orderly enough?
That is very individual. A possible answer is that if you feel able to welcome unexpected guests at any moment without feeling the slightest need to explain or justify the condition of your house, then your house must be orderly enough.

Creating order is not my problem, but maintaining it seems to be impossible. Sometimes it drives me crazy. How can I change that?
How long does the order last? What causes the disorder? For instance, if every evening before going to bed, everybody in the house looks around the common spaces – such as kitchen, living room and bathroom – to check what belongs to them, and then removes it, you will have a basic order in the morning. It helps if you put papers such as newspapers or bills where they belong. In the kitchen put whatever is not needed back where it belongs. You can also make a point of observing your movements carefully for a certain period of time. What do I do with something I pick up? You could also make a special effort to keep one place neat and tidy for about two weeks. This may even become a new and useful habit.

I have fallen behind with so many things in my home that I don't believe I will ever be able to have order again. And even if I start, when I finished with the last room the rest are back to the same condition they were before.

And then I haven't even touched the attic or the cellar. Where and how can I possibly start?

If it's as bad as that, I would suggest you forget about the cellar and the attic at present. Of course, the aim is to have order and to pick up everything that's lying about, but the priority is now to find a rhythm in your daily life. The most important things are that there is food on the table, and that everybody has something clean to wear. It should also at least be sufficiently clean to avoid being invaded by vermin. Then make sure the bills are paid so that you have electricity, water, telephone and insurance.

To manage all these things you need to have a daily or weekly rhythm. Such regularity will support you. Once you have found a rhythm that suits you and are able to keep to it, you should then be able to slowly manage the rest of your household. You may have a friend in a similar situation who may be able to help you. You will then be able to support each other.

How can I decide what I should keep, what to throw away, or what to give away?

It is best not to start with the question of whether you still needed or not, but rather, why you want to keep it. Does it make you feel guilty? What does it mean to you? Does it give you joy or is it a burden? Don't keep anything that does not give you joy.

My house seems to be getting fuller all the time. How can I change it?

Maintaining order often starts with shopping. Ask yourself in the store whether you really need what you have in your hand right now? Do you want to buy it simply because it is so cheap? Have you become the rubbish bin of the family and does everything the others don't want any more land with you? If this is so, you need to learn to say, No. You can also decide that whenever something new comes into the house, something old has to go. My husband had this thing with shoes. Whenever he bought a new pair, I wanted to know what would happen to the old pair. Then the following kind of conversation would ensue.

'So we can get rid of this old pair?'

'No, I'd like to keep those for cleaning.'

'But you already have a pair for cleaning.'

'Yes but those I'd like to use for gardening.'

'That means we can get rid of the old gardening shoes.'

'I could use those if I need to dig in the garden after the rain.'

My friend's house always seems to be a little bit disorderly, yet I never have the feeling that it is really so. Why does my own disorder feel distinctly like disorder?

I believe it has to do with a basic order and care. One senses when a house is well looked after. Just as one can sense chaos when everything has been stuffed under the bed or into the cupboard hastily, in order to create an image of order, you can feel order in a kitchen if the work-surfaces are completely covered and the floor is full of toys. At first glance this may create an impression of disorder, but it can probably all be cleared in a few minutes.

Is it possible to teach an experienced person to do something the way I would like to have it done?

I once needed to urgently find a trained person for a day-time cleaning job in a laboratory. Students could not do this work, as they worked mostly early in the mornings before going to school. So I asked a young Puerto Rican woman who had applied for job earlier. I asked her husband – she could hardly speak German – to bring her to my house so that I could teach her how to clean. He assured me that she had worked for many cleaning companies, but I insisted that she came to my house for instruction.

It turned out to be a very difficult task because she insisted on knowing everything already and took nothing on board of what I was trying to teach her. I showed her the kitchen sink, gave her a cleaning agent and asked her to clean it.

'Where Vim?' came her question in return.

I told her that she should use the cleaning agent I had given to her. She put a few splashes on the surface, whoosh, whoosh and she was finished, without having touched even a corner or the faucet.

'It's not clean,' I said and showed her what she had missed.

She repeated the process, but nothing changed. I showed her how to do the vacuuming; here again, she ignored my indications and vacu-umed in a fan shape around her. Out of sheer desperation, I said, 'And now I will show you how to clean a toilet.'

I took my tools and my cleaning materials, knelt down in front of the toilet and began to clean it thoroughly. She became very quiet, and I felt that her whole attention was focused on the work. We did not speak a word, and when I had finished, she said with shining eyes, 'You wonderful cleaning, I clean so like you.'

I asked her again to clean the kitchen sink, and I did not have to say anything anymore: she knew how to clean. She stayed for six months, and was very popular and held in high esteem.

8. Rhythm

A healthy rhythm is vital and needs to be maintained. The whole universe is imbued with rhythm. And where there is rhythm, there is also order.

When I introduce someone to the job, I always point out the importance of rhythm. Rhythmic movement does not tire. If we work only with muscles and willpower, the movements will tense up shoulders and neck, strain the body and be tiring.

If we fully connect with our work and immerse ourselves entirely in a particular activity, we will find its own particular rhythm. Thus our work becomes easier, as if we are receiving help. Sometime our tiredness will vanish and we are overcome by a feeling of contentment and joy. We may even have the feeling that we have been gifted extra time.

In many cultures rhythms defined daily routines. As a child in South Africa, I saw the local people singing to the rhythm of a caller when excavating pits. Sometimes, if an 'efficient' white foreman reckoned the pace was too slow and asked them to stop singing, the work often came to a standstill.

At a street corner in Johannesburg there was a small black shoeshine boy. I loved watching him in his work, which he did with joy, always singing funny, lively ditties. One day a priest was having his shoes cleaned, and asked the boy why he did not sing the praises of the Lord while he worked. Immediately the boy sang a church hymn. After two verses he stopped and said, 'No, master, at that pace I shall never finish.'

We often speak of a 'healthy rhythm.' Rhythm must not be confused with routine. Everything that repeats itself in life can become routine, and nothing is more oppressing than daily work done routinely and monotonously. Emphasis on rhythm, on the other hand, adds colour to life and makes work easier.

Rhythm in everyday life, in the little things, is particularly important because we are nowadays often exposed arrhythmic disorder or confusion. Sometimes it is very hard to create clearly structured rhythms out of which order can evolve. We have to strive constantly to distinguish the essential from the inessential, and we have to ensure that we concentrate on what is important without being sidetracked into distractions.

Each of us must of course decide how to organise our household, so that we feel at ease, without being rushed from one task to the other. If I know I do my laundry on a Wednesday, I need not worry about it during the rest of the week. There is a rhythm for the household, and there is a rhythm for life. In contrast to rigidly enforced routine, rhythm is flexible and alive, supporting us.

A steady rhythm is particularly important as long as the children are still young. Getting up, going to school or work, taking meals, doing homework, doing sport, attending music lessons, taking-care of pets, brushing teeth, washing, reading stories, going to bed are all part of the life of a family household. To cope with all this, we need rhythm, and the better the rhythm is maintained, the better everything flows.

Food

I once lived in a house in which I could tell the day of the week by the scent the neighbour' hallway. Monday was washday, and minestrone was on the menu. Tuesday was ironing day, and there was fruit pie, depending on the season. On Wednesdays, the entire apartment was thoroughly vacuumed, accompanied by the smell of pizza, and so on. Many people find that such a rhythm makes life easier.

When planning a rhythm, first consider everything related to food. Shopping (with or without a shopping list) is followed by unpacking and storing. Clearing up, washing up, separating and disposal of waste, all of this is part of cooking. If there is a vegetable garden, the annual rhythm also has to be taken into account – sowing, planting, weeding, watering and harvesting. (It is good if children can experience all these processes.)

For groceries we need space; for cooking we need pots and pans and so on; for a meal we need tables, chairs, tablecloths, plates and cutlery. All these things need space and care. The kitchen has always been – and is often still today – the heart of the house. Since this is the place in which we do a great part of our work, it should be set up as well and comfortably as possible. Things that we do not need often should not take up valuable workspace and annoy us. It is good to check from time to time, if everything taking up space in the kitchen really belongs there.

When my children still lived at home, it was a rule that the boys and men were responsible for the dishes at noon and the women in the evening. The boys swept the floor one day and the girls did it on the next day. This rhythm was so ingrained that the visiting children took part in it as a matter of course, in order to be able to quickly get down to play.

Clothing

The word 'clothing' brings a whole range of things to mind: shopping (or even sewing oneself), washing, treating stains, mending, ironing, folding, storing and – most importantly – disposing. Not many people patch or darn nowadays, yet sewing on buttons, mending tears, taking up hems or replacing zips all need to be done. How and when do we find time for all this?

I have a small sewing kit near my ironing board so that I can do the repairs when they appear. My sister's family always knew where to find their missing clothes, for her mending basket was always full. I have many friends who knit while having a chat – but they rarely darn, though it would be a good opportunity. A friend of mine always takes something to sew or to darn when waiting at the doctor or dentist.

Stains can most easily be removed when fresh. Later on, soaking Can help. Look at freshly laundered clothes before ironing or when folding. Don't ironed in a stain; then it will often be impossible to get rid of.

Ironing can be combined with listening to music, audio books, lectures, or watching something on television. Once the children are old enough, they can learn to iron themselves; I stopped ironing for my children quite early, and even my husband has learned to iron.

There are some people who like to display their laundry for days in the living room. If the ironing is not away promptly someone will start rummaging through the piles, often messing up the other garments.

As important as acquiring new clothing is, so is its disposal. How many clothes does a person need? When has a garment had its day? How long should I keep the children's clothes, and is it worth keeping everything I've ever bought or been given, even if no one will ever wear it again? Or what about the beautiful dresses that will never fit me again? Is it worth being burdened by the many things filling closets, basements and lofts – often without ever being noticed? Is that worthy of these things that have served us at some time and given us joy?

A good opportunity to take a careful look at our clothes is when we store our winter clothes and take out our summer clothes again. If we see something we have not worn for years, would now not be an opportunity to part with it? Or, if that is still too difficult, we can choose this moment to store the garment, saying, 'If I do not wear you this summer, then you may go when winter comes.'

Then there is the bed linen. Is there a rhythm for changing and washing it? Is there enough to freshly make the bed before the old linen has been washed and dried?

Tidying and cleaning

In earlier times hospitality was a sacred task. This is no longer the case today because people are too ashamed to receive guests, or because it causes too much stress to tidy up. In extreme cases this can even lead to social isolation.

Again, it is important to find a rhythm tailored to your needs and the needs of the family. Most importantly, it must suit everyone. Some people like to do some clean every day – the bathroom on Mondays, the living room on Tuesdays, the bedrooms on Wednesdays, and so on. If it works, stick to that.

For me, doing all the cleaning once a week works well. To live with the thought, 'I'll do the housework when I have time,' would leave me constantly feeling that something was weighing on my shoulders. When my children were still at home, we used to always clean on a

Thursday afternoon because they had no school then. Since both my husband and I were self-employed, we did not accept any jobs on these afternoons. The house was divided into four areas. Bathroom and toilet were my task; my daughter dusted and looked after the plants; my son vacuumed and wiped the hallway and stairwell, and my husband vacuumed all floors downstairs and our bedroom. The children were responsible for their own bedrooms, and the kitchen was cleaned every day. We never needed more than an hour per person, which means a total of four hours per week. If, for some reason, someone could not be there on a Thursday, they had to do their work beforehand on Wednesday (experience taught me that catching up rarely works).

If someone came to visit on Wednesday night, there may have been an occasional bit of fluff or dust in a corner somewhere, but it did not bother me, because I knew that it would be cleaned on Thursday. Obviously, if something was disturbing it was immediately wiped away, but otherwise I had the rest of the week off.

A course participant told me that she had found a way to encourage her young daughter to tidy up. She would stand in the doorway and say, 'I see something, and it is blue.' Then all the blue items were found and put away. As the little girl wanted to tidy up another colour straightaway, the room was tidied in no time at all.

Dishes should immediately either be washed by hand or stacked in the dishwasher. In this way dishes are cleaned faster, using less water, detergent and time. Dirty dishes left lying about have an effect on the atmosphere, not only in the kitchen. Avoid leaving dirty dishes overnight, especially in summer when insects may be a problem.

I like to get up early in the morning, because this when I have time to myself. There are no phone calls or interruptions, just peace and quiet. I can meditate, read, write, even mend a little, or tidy up something in peace. This time is sacred to me, and a tidy kitchen is essential when I put on the kettle.

A friend from America told me that she always started her morning washing up coffee cups and other things her family had used after dinner. For her it was an arrival in the reality of everyday life. I assured her that I had no intention of changing what works well for her, especially if it was done with pleasure. When I saw her a year later she beamed and said, 'Everything has changed. Everyone in the house washes their dishes in the evening and puts them away. For months now I've also been enjoying the stillness of the morning, and have caught up with many things that I'd been wanting to do for a long time.'

Another thing I care about is my bathroom sink. After brushing my teeth, I wipe it immediately with a soft cloth. As I clean it every day, I do not need a cleaning agent and it only takes thirty seconds. When I get up I always see a brilliantly white sink, which gives me an unmissable feeling of freshness.

Personal hygiene, too, is part of cleaning. Do the children have a rhythm for having a bath, for washing their hair and having their nails cut? Pets also need cleaning and care, brushing, delousing and washing. Cat litter and food bowls have to be cleaned. On which day of the week are these tasks done?

Once a healthy rhythm is established it is possible to keep on top of the various tasks, and the household will run with less effort and struggle.

Household maintenance

Routine maintenance is something that we can do ourselves, while major repairs, renovations or servicing needs to be carried out by specialists. While we are cleaning, we should check that all the bulbs work, and whether or not the vacuum cleaner sounds and smells right. A loose electrical contact should be repaired before it causes a short circuit. We can learn to rely on our senses, especially the sense of smell. Mice, for example, can be smelt, even if they can't be seen. The smell from the drain can tell us that something is wrong, and a smell of gas will alert us to a leak. Our sense of sight warns us of other things: calcium deposits behind the toilet bowl indicating a damaged seal; lime deposits in the basin, may indicate a leaking tap or connection pipe; an unexplained water stain reveals a leak. Mould points to excessive moisture or inadequate ventilation. These kind of problems are all maintenance that should be carried out immediately.

Having a rhythm to replace the vacuum cleaner bag, can avoid damage, especially if different people use the cleaner at different times. Filters need to be replaced less often, but must not be forgotten.

Cleaning gutters, removing moss from the garden tiles, re-painting, descaling and servicing boilers, painting window frames and such like all need their own rhythm, and often a professional.

Lifestyle habits

All that sounds like a tall order. But many things can become healthy habits when practised regularly, like putting your bunch of keys or hanging your coat in the right place as soon as you come home. It can be of great benefit, if at all possible, to find a time and a place for everything. Interim storage and temporary solutions take more time in the long run.

The things I put at the bottom of the stairs to take up later, should really be upstairs by the evening. But please don't think that everything works like clockwork for me. Life always has surprises for us in store, but since I'm in control of my household (and not vice versa), I neither feel forced, nor do I have to prove anything to anyone. During the summer there are always some things left undone, because then the garden is a priority. I try my best to keep track and judge when to intervene before things get out of hand.

It can be a good idea to take time to go through the house making a list. How does it look? What needs to be immediately addressed or changed, and what can wait? Don't lose heart straight away. That first step is needed. It is always best to determine where the main problem lies, and where to begin. Which habits do we want to change? If we live in a family, it is not just about our personal habits, but also about the general ones that have crept into the household. Teamwork is necessary, as well as clear communication; family meetings are needed to reach agreements. Organising such things is obviously not everybody's strength, but it works wonderfully well in many families.

Ultimately, each of us must also decide what is important to us. If there are things that seem to be important only for you, don't bother the whole family with them. In our family it was the flowers: I was the one who noticed them, so I looked after them.

My biggest challenge was my inability to maintain order. I had no trouble creating order, but to keep it was almost impossible. When

I arrived in Switzerland newly married, I made a big mistake when I put a chair into the bedroom. Eventually I discovered the connection between my empty closet and the pile of clothes on the back of the chair. But a change came about only when I found it annoying having to iron or wash a piece of clothing every time I wanted to wear something. I took the chair out of the bedroom, and changed in the bathroom. Here I could put the clothes where they belonged – in the laundry basket, on the hook for airing, or hung up so that I could wear them again.

Like many people, I had trouble with paperwork. I bought a small cabinet with six drawers, labelling them 'bank, invoices, house, tax, correspondence, husband's'. I open all letters immediately and sort them into the drawers. Envelopes, catalogues, etc. go straight into the wastepaper basket. The invoices are paid once a month.

An important evening ritual is to look at all the common spaces – kitchen, living and dining room, hallway and bathroom – and find the personal things that do not belong there. If each person looks after his own bag, sweater, magazine, musical instrument, then there is order. This is a wonderful habit that contributes much to the common good and gives a good start to the next day.

I'm still discovering new reasons why I am disorderly. Through repetition it becomes easier to keep a tidy environment, the whole family can develop new skills. If at an early age children regularly repeat such tasks in certain rhythms, their willpower, commitment and reliability are strengthened.

9. Home Life and Growing Children

*The joy of children in and with their environment, must therefore be
counted among the forces that build and shape the physical organs.
They need teachers that look and act with happiness and, most of
all, with honest unaffected love. Such a love that streams, as it were,
with warmth through the physical environment of the children may
be said to literally 'hatch' the forms of the physical organs.*

*The children who live in such an atmosphere of love and
warmth, and who have around them truly good examples to
imitate, are living in their proper element. One should thus strictly
guard against anything being done in the children's presence that
they should not imitate.*

Rudolf Steiner[1]

The pressure on parenthood

Peer pressure – wanting to belong – is no longer found only among
teenagers, but can be experienced in all walks of life. Mothers who have
studied want to practice their profession. Others feel overwhelmed by
the myriad of everyday tasks at home, and feel the need to unfold themselves, to follow their own interests or do voluntary work.

Many feel exasperated because they believe they first half to sort out
and organise their practical life before they can be free to think about any
kind of self development. We should not wait until our affairs are in order
before embarking on self development or a spiritual path, for nothing is
ever permanently sort it out and new problems are always cropping up.
A spiritual path may actually help to find better solutions to everyday
problems, for it helps us to be stronger, more patient, sensible and wise.

Yet striving to find balance between self development and the necessities of daily life is actually already a step in self development.

As parents we always try to do our best for our children, but we all make mistakes. However, we should not become disheartened, and should certainly not feel that everything we have done so far was wrong. It is never too late to learn something new or to change certain habits.

There are so many (often contradictory) self-help books that even this can add pressure and make us feel even more overwhelmed. To satisfy every material wish of our children is not the most important thing. Most children sense their parents sincere striving, and this helps children thrive.

Educating children will always be like walking on a tightrope. We also need a lot of patience with them as well as with ourselves. Children simply need the time they need. Their path to adulthood is one of transformation and development that cannot be hurried. It is also important not to set our standards and ideals unreasonably high. Otherwise we shall be frustrated and disappointed having overtaxed ourselves and our children.

We also know the wonderful moments when our child has been to friends and their mother calls to tell us what a polite child we have, who helped everywhere during a weekend visit. Even if it's not always like that at home, after a call like that we know that our children have learned something.

This book is not about child development. Nevertheless, running seminars for more than twenty years made me realise how much anguish could be avoided if young parents knew more about the importance of child development. So I would like to mention a few aspects as well as bringing examples from my own experience.

Free play

Thomas Marti – a father of three and lecturer in anthroposophical education in Germany – identified free play as a key element of early years education.

While at play children have no awareness that they are learning social skills through free play, and the emphasis here is on free play as opposed to organised play activity. These social skills include role play, problem solving, conversation, crisis management, innovation and creativity. Their imagination is simply enhanced by dealing with situations which they freely act out. These abilities – called soft skills which become the basis of personality – are needed right up to the elite of corporate boardrooms or of politics. More people are needed in these situations who are strong in a crisis, and can develop practical solutions rather than thought-out schemes.[2]

Parents often think they have to teach their children how and what to play, children have all this as a treasure within them. As parents we should rather try to remove any obstacles which stop children from discovering themselves and their surroundings which they do by simply exploring, trying things out and learning through doing. Ideally this should be done in an environment which is stimulating, but at the same time protected and protective.

Children are still open to what lives in their surroundings; they take it all in, almost without filtering, and let it work upon them. They are inwardly totally taken up by imitation, taking in what the world has to offer, and what adults show through example. Children want to be like the adults, and what they see, experience and imitate has far-reaching consequences.

Time was in short supply shortly after the founding of my company. On many occasions I simply did not have time for long walks or children's games. Instead I always tried to involve my children in my activities. It was important to know they were nearby while I was seeing to the necessary chores as conscientiously as possible.

A young man once came to me wanting to learn some basic household skills. He told me how much as a young child he had wanted to help his mother with her chores, but she always said it was easier for her to do it herself, and that he should go and play instead. Involving our youngsters in our household tasks ensures that the opportunity to learn basic skills is not missed.

In the early years children develop their organs, particularly the brain. The neurons connect as a result of children's activities. Therefore it is so important to act in the right way and create the right environment for our children. We need to ensure they have the right level of stimulation, seeking a nourishing balance that neither overpowers nor dulls. Everything we do around our children is absorbed by them and has consequences. Not only what we say, but how we say it, how we touch children while changing their diaper (nappy), how we look at them when we feed them. They have a completely different experience if they play outside or if they are set down in front of the television. (Research has shown that not only the content of TV programmes, but also the passive posture and focused gaze can have long lasting negative effects.[3]) Children have a natural inclination to be active, to move about and to discover the real world.

Imitation

Education starts at home, in the cradle as it were. I spent most time with my children in the kitchen. There they were able to fulfil little tasks, develop confidence in themselves and feel that they, too, can achieve something, thus contributing to the community.

In the first seven years children are in the age of imitation. They observe and imitate. They see us working with love (or not). Once, after a domestic dispute in the garage (so the children would not hear it) I entered the kitchen to continue doing the dishes. My four-year-old daughter sat at the table painting. As soon as I started working she stopped painting and looked at me intently. After a bit I asked her why she did not continue with her painting. She replied, 'You work much faster when you're angry, don't you?'

At this age children sense everything in their environment, not only what adults do, but also how they think and feel. This, of course, creates a challenge for parents who at all times have to try to be worthy of imitation. How and what children imitate so intensely at this age lays the foundation for social freedom in later life.

Support and patience

When I am in the tram, bus or train, I often notice how roughly some parents tend to handle their children. I sense the parents' impatience and frustration that seem to be a reason for their not coping. A two-year-old is slapped because she has dropped an apple by mistake, or is dragged along impatiently, while wanting to observe some little creature crawling on the ground.

It is important to allow children the time to observe, explore and imitate, and not to rush them or try to accelerate their development through stimulation or exercises. They will sit, stand and walk once they are ready. Every bit of progress they make through their own effort provides an opportunity to exercise their will. Ignoring their pace deprives them of a healthy development.

We can begin creating such moments in everyday chores like changing diapers. This can become an intense time of sharing and bonding, through patient, loving gestures. Instead of giving the baby a toy to distract it, we can consciously make eye contact, gently touch her and talk to her. Many everyday activities we do with our children can become precious moments of sharing.

At the age of about two children begin to imitate our actions. When they see us tackling our daily tasks joyfully, they will imitate the way we handle our utensils. This applies not only to pots and wooden spoons, but also to dustpan and brush, vacuum cleaner, mop or clothes pegs. Although children do not yet understand the meaning of work, they imitate what they see. Father washing his car or repairing something in the house is something fascinating, and demands a similar action on their part. They want to cook, bake, clean, wash, simply because their parent does it. But it can also happen that while playing in the sandbox, they throw a plastic pot against the wall of the neighbouring house and, when reprimanded, quite calmly claim, 'My mummy does the same when she is angry.'

A special air surrounds a person who works with total surrender and devotion to the task at hand. This fascinates children and they want to help, they want to participate, sometimes just look or be close by. The gestures and whole demeanour of such an adult takes on a pedagogical and healing aspect.

Then at about three years imagination blossoms, and all of a sudden a bucket is not something for cleaning, but becomes a fireman's helmet. At that age children start saying 'No!' to many things, and are unable to understand why they aren't allowed to turn the chair around, if it needs it to become a truck. Children do not need many toys at this age, because they are able to transform anything around them into what they need. They can suddenly become a grunting dinosaur in the kitchen, or a cat that only wants to drink its milk from a saucer. They discover the world around him through personal experience, and do not need educational toys. Simply allowing our children to play is a gift for life.

As children become older, they show more personal initiative. That is the time for us as parents to step back and patiently support and encourage their efforts. Especially in the kitchen, children can develop skills and at the same time participate in activities that support family life. To tell them to go and play when they offer help is a mistake.

If we as parents endeavour to sense the deeper needs of our children, we will not only understand our children much better, but will also understand ourselves. This will help us to discover the deeper meaning of parenthood and enable us to offer our children a suitable environment in which to grow up. There are, of course, times when our children are more difficult, and challenge our patience. Personally, I have found consolation in the knowledge that my children are surrounded by helpful beings such as their guardian angels.

The time that we invest in our children is certainly the biggest and most secure investment we will ever make: we invest in the future of humanity. The more we realise the importance of these moments spent with our children, the easier it will become for us to find the necessary inner calm to enjoy them. We don't really lose time through these activities, but often gain time. If children feel noticed and taken seriously, they will feel secure and content, and be less needy of our attention. They will develop a lively interest in their environment if children can experience their mother being content when cleaning or ironing. Later when asked to take on some household tasks, they'll do so without too much trouble.

Children naturally have perseverance, concentration, and strength.

We can support them allowing them to experiment, and we should not dampen their enthusiasm by impatiently wanting to show them how to do it the right way, or to trying to train them to do things the way we want them done. Children should not miss certain phases in their development because of our impatience. They will learn through example and imitation, through rhythm and repetition. If we praise them for something they have done, this should be genuine and not be corrected or improved afterwards. If a little bit is unfinished, we can show them how to do it, and then tell them, 'Now it is really perfect!' Constant nagging and finding fault will discourage them, making them feel that they are not up to the task. They must be allowed to learn through trial and error.

At kindergarten age my son never wanted to tie his shoelaces and always simply said, 'I can't do it.' So every time I tied the laces for him I did the gesture very carefully and commented what I was doing. He looked very closely, but never wanted to try. One day, while he was playing with a beautiful red ribbon, I said, 'Come and help me. I would like to have a lovely bow tied around my wrist.' Without the slightest hesitation he tied the bowl and then said in total astonishment, 'But Mummy, that is exactly like tying shoelaces.' His kindergarten teacher told me that from that day he would rush to the changing rooms after class, to help all the children who could not yet tie their shoelaces.

Rhythm, and coming to agreements

There are universal principles that underlie all child development, whatever the individual differences. Among these principles are that children need adults worthy of imitation and they need rhythm which supports health.

Impatience is perhaps the biggest weakness of most parents. Children need their own time to develop, and we support our children best if everything is repeated in a rhythmic way. Be it by repeating rhymes, songs, finger games, or in the daily and weekly rhythms of preparing meals, laying the table, washing the dishes or the little rituals of getting ready for bed and the bedtime story. Experiencing rhythm at home, in the kindergarten and in school, gives children confidence in life.

Recurring events give them a feeling of security. Without points of reference, children lose their sense of direction causing insecurity and anxiety.

While my children will were still quite small, I tried to arrange most of my work on a Thursday when I would leave the house before [7] and only return about 8 pm, just in time to say good night. On Wednesday evenings Emily, an old friend, would come to us. The children knew that it would be Emily who would wake them in the morning, spend the whole day with them and put them to bed in the evening.

Yet there was always something special about Thursdays, because at lunch, when I was able to briefly return home, the table was laid in a festive manner with a white tablecloth, flowers and candles, and there was a special meal and always ice cream for dessert. To start the meal we had a special song accompanied by gestures that was only sung on Thursdays. We kept this rhythm for well over two years. Later the children always used to remind me of this weekly day of festivity, but they did not remember that I was away for the whole day.

Going to bed and getting up

Many parents of young children dread bedtime. It can be exhausting and very trying on the nerves. They can scream and sometimes cry themselves to sleep. A young mother once told me that their young son was difficult when it came to going to bed, and that she would provoke him until he became so furious and would start screaming. She found this was the easiest way to exhaust him so that he would finally go to sleep. I suggested she should try and remember what it had felt like to her, if as a child she had to go to bed without a problem having been solved, crying herself to sleep. If we remember this, we will try to put our children to bed in a way that allows them to go to sleep in a harmonious and peaceful way.

Going to bed can be a ritual, a very special moment where habits are formed that last a lifetime. This is where my children learned to sort out the toys they had played with and the clothes they had worn. Of course, I did it all, but they were always included and participated, especially in making decisions, like what goes into the laundry basket, what do we hang out to air, and what can we wear again tomorrow? Socks were very important. Whenever a sock was peeled off and left in a 'ball', I demonstrated how a sock should be untangled and flattened before being placed in the laundry basket, saying, 'Mummy never washes any "balls".'

Another important rule was that I never told the bedtime story unless the room was tidy. This was the last moment of the day when we could still do something together, and my children always helped because storytelling was very important to them. Of course, we didn't clear away the things that they still wanted to continue playing with the next day. The more interesting the story that I was telling, the earlier they were ready to tidy up and go to bed. (Our guests were often surprised when our children came in to remind us of their bedtime.) On the other hand, sometimes in the summer vacations they enjoyed playing outside so much that story time lasted barely five minutes.

We lit a candle for our bedtime story, we spoke about the events of the day, and also about their grandfather who had passed away, because he was always invited to share our story. After the story we would say a prayer together, and then they took turns in putting out the candle.

When they got up in the morning I always accompanied the sequence of events with a commentary, 'Open the window. Open up the bed. Then wash face and hands. Get dressed. Make the bed. Close the window.' When they are still young, children simply accept these things as a natural part of the daily routine, and this makes things easier when they are older. Of course, during puberty, certain things seem to get lost for a while, but what was done regularly over a period of time seems, in my experience, to come back.

Mealtimes

Some families never share a communal meal except when they have visitors. Everybody comes and fetches something when they feel hungry, open a can, or slip something into the microwave. As well as an unbalanced diet being unhealthy, an important element of family life is lost. If we do not share our meals, when do exchanges take place? Do we still take an interest in each other's well-being?

With my children we made a special game of laying the table. As a child, I had never experienced my mother sharing a whole meal with us in peace and quiet; there was always some reason for her to get up. Even as a small child this used to disturb me, and I felt sorry for her. Already then I decided that if ever I had children, I would share my meals with my family from beginning to end. So, we took great care in laying the table and always checked if something was missing – we even had a cloth and little bowl of water, in case something needed wiping up. My children made a little game of this: whenever I turned away they would quickly hide something and then looked at me expectantly to see if I would notice what was missing.

We also had an agreement that the beginning of the meals would be quiet and without too much chatter, to allow us to concentrate on the food. When they were older, another important agreement was only 'gold piece' conversations were allowed at table, and no 'toad' talk (from Grimm's tale of The Three Little Men in the Wood). For the latter we would arrange a special time. If my daughter came home quite excited and wanted to tell me about how stupid this and that person was, I would immediately ask, 'Is it a gold piece or a toad that is going to come from your mouth now?' The toad would have to wait until after lunch and by then was often forgotten.

The privilege of having a full-time parent has become quite rare, as both parents often go out to work. It is important that we try to make arrangements where children can experience at least some consistency of carers. Too many changes are unsettling, making it difficult for them to bond.

Developing a sense of responsibility

We can begin to encourage a sense of responsibility in children around the age of 10 to 12. If youngsters learn to take full responsibility for what they do, it will strengthen their will. Often young people do not seem to find the will power to do what they want to do and know they should do. The task of parents and teachers is to support teenagers in developing their will, so that their will may serve them, rather than overpowering them.

Young people like to talk about freedom but it is important to teach them the difference between freedom and impulsiveness, and between freedom and taking liberties. Freedom comes with responsibility, though that is difficult for a teenager to understand or accept. If we can show through examples, without being moralising, that every decision has consequences, it will help them to take responsibility for what they do. The word morality has a negative ring, yet it is vital that young people develop a sense for it.

In our family we tried to build up a culture of agreements. We discussed certain chores that were to be done in the family, and then we agreed on who should take each one on. Additional tasks were offered to the children as paid jobs, for instance, mowing the lawn for five francs. The agreement was that the lawn should be mowed once a week. If a week was skipped, and it needed quite a bit more time to do the same job, the pay was still five francs, which of course encouraged weekly mowing.

Another agreement was that the bedding should be changed every second week. I did the laundry and put the clean bed linen on their beds which they then had to make themselves. Occasionally they chose to sleep on the mattress under a duvet without a cover. I told them that if the duvet or mattress got dirty because their bed wasn't made, they would have to pay the dry cleaning. The choice was theirs, as were the consequences.

Closed for reconstruction: adolescence

At puberty some of the things we as parents cultivated with love and perseverance seem suddenly to disappear, and everything that was self-evident is questioned. For growing youngsters it can be a time of reconstruction, a new beginning. All of a sudden a sticker appears on their door: No entry. It is like a sign saying, 'Closed for reconstruction.'

Parents sometimes feel helpless and filled with self doubt. It can help to reflect on your own puberty. Was it so bad? How long did it last? Can we recall those moments of indescribable loneliness and helplessness, the difficulty of communicating with adults who always seem to take everything as a personal attack or criticism? Perhaps we can remember how sensitive we were, convinced that no one could understand us or take us seriously.

Our adolescence came and went – and so will that of our children. There will be times we reach our limits and come close to despair. My daughter and I once looked at each other, both crying, when I heard myself say, 'Just as new and unsettling as it is for you to experience adolescence, it is to me to have an adolescent daughter. Let us learn together, and try to treat each other with respect.'

Part of growing up is the need to experience what it would feel like to live in total chaos. Experimenting is part of gaining independence, searching for the own individuality. They need to decide for themselves which rules they are willing to accept or not. They want to try out different systems; they also try to create a distance, to establish a border between themselves and their parents. Sometimes they purposely do exactly the opposite of what they have learned from their parents, for instance, leaving a heap of dirty laundry on the floor, or letting the dirty dishes pile up until there are no more clean plates available. It can come as a surprise to us later when they move into their own place, they again know exactly what to do.

Children have to learn how to arrange their time between discos, parties and homework, sport and recreation. It can of course happen that somehow they don't seem to find time for making order in their rooms or doing other chores around the house. If in this situation parents put too much pressure on them, it can lead to rebellion, protest. On the other hand expecting them to be independent when they are too young, can overtax them, and can later express itself in disorder not only in space but also in organising their time.

I did not always find it easy, but resolved never to humiliate my children or verbally abuse them. I considered it important that we should stick to our agreements. One of these agreements was that I said I would never wash socks that were left as 'balls'. For a long time everybody stuck to this agreement and the socks were neatly unravelled before they landed in the laundry basket. When my son was about 13 I discovered 'balls' in the laundry basket. I decided not to say a word, knowing that the more 'balls' there were in the basket, the less clean socks would be found in his drawer. About ten days later, one morning before school, I heard a drawer open, slammed close, followed by an exasperated, 'There are no clean socks in this dump.' I innocently asked him whether his problem might have anything to do with the 'balls' in the laundry basket. He didn't say a word, but all the socks were unravelled. There was no repetition after that, simply because he understood that I was going to stick to our agreement.

Another agreement that I had with the children was that the kitchen was always to be tidy when I got up in the morning which was usually about 5 am. The children were allowed to invite friends, make snacks and use the kitchen as they pleased as long as it was orderly in the morning. In all the years as teenagers I only once had to wake my son and my daughter at 5 am to clear the kitchen.

Love and trust

Although the children can be very independent and headstrong at this age they still need the security of knowing that we love them the way they are and that we trust them. Trusting our teenagers is having faith that what we had given them as children will now help them to develop into healthy young adults.

This is not an easy time. There are moments of criticism, reproaches, waking up to reality when they discover that their parents aren't quite such perfect people as they thought. In their innermost being young people long for a good world, a safe place. They even wish to help to make it a better place and sometimes ask how they can go about it. They often ask questions about justice, fairness, tolerance and freedom. If we fail to understand deeper reasons for their criticism we discourage them in their hope of making things better. They need our confidence and our trust even when they are relentless in their arguments and in their attempts to show us how in adequate our own reasoning seem to them.

There is an aphoristic text by Rudolf Steiner about the archetypal human being. True interest in our children may lead us to discover their archetypal being.

Create for yourself a new, indomitable perception of faithfulness. What is usually called faithfulness passes so quickly. Let this be your faithfulness. You will experience fleeting moments with the other person when they appear as if filled, radiating with the archetype of their spirit. And then there will be other times – long periods – when that light of the human being is darkened. But learn to say to yourself at such times, 'The spirit makes me strong. I recall the archetype, for I saw it once. No illusion, no deception shall rob me of that.' Strive continually for the image that you saw. This striving is faithfulness. Striving thus for faithfulness, we shall be close to one another, as if endowed with the protective powers of angels.[4]

Sometimes, when it was really difficult to maintain this faith, I would look at photographs of my children when they were young looking at me with their unlimited love and trust.

In Marianne Williamson's book, *A Return to Love*, there is a wonderful passage often (but erroneously) attributed to Nelson Mandela's inaugural address. I wish every young person would take these words to heart.

Our deepest fear is not that we are inadequate. Our deepest fear is that we are powerful beyond measure. It is our light, not our darkness that most frightens us. We ask ourselves, who am I to be brilliant, gorgeous, talented, and fabulous? Actually, who are you not to be? You are a child of God. Your playing small does not serve the world. There is nothing enlightened about shrinking so that other people won't feel insecure around you. We are all meant to shine, as children do. We were born to make manifest the glory of God that is within us. It's not just in some of us; it's in everyone. And as we let our own light shine, we unconsciously give other people permission to do the same. As we are liberated from our own fear, our presence automatically liberates others.[5]

Meaningful work

During a workshop one of the participants said that she hoped I could teach her to have fun while she cleans. She looked a little bit disappointed when I told her that I was not interested in teaching people to have fun. To me it is much more important to experience joy while cleaning and caring. Fun passes, but joy is more lasting. To experience joy in household activities we need to understand their deeper meaning and purpose. Why do we clean? What ideal do we follow while we do our household duties?

Without cleaning our home and family are in danger of falling apart. What distinguishes a house from a home is the care we put into it. The home remains the cradle of humanity, and if we believe that our children are indifferent to the conditions in which they live, we are fooling ourselves. Sometimes children are profoundly ashamed of and humiliated by the conditions at home but hide this under the guise of nonchalance, even pretending it is cool by making silly excuses. A student justified the filth in his bedroom in a student house with, 'Everything you see is organic, pure nature.'

During a workshop a young man was particularly interested in everything I had to say, and wanted to try out everything I demonstrated. He asked a lot of questions and took a lot of notes. Four weeks later I received the following email.

> Immediately after you started talking, I became aware of
> the state that my children and I were living in. I am 35 years
> old and a single working father of three boys aged eight,
> ten and twelve. Ever since my wife left us almost a year ago,
> we have hardly done the bare necessities around the house.
> Coming home after the workshop, I felt so ashamed and
> disgusted about the state we lived in that I firmly resolved
> to tidy and clean something in the house every day, even
> if only for 10 minutes, until everything would be ordered
> and cared for. I have done this for the last four weeks.
> After the first week, the boys of their own accord offered
> to help. Yesterday morning we managed the final touches,
> and our house is now tidy and clean. This morning I baked

something special for our Sunday breakfast and while we were at the table my twelve-year-old son said, 'Thank you, daddy. We now have a home again.'

Even if we don't manage it all the time, it is good for children to experience the difference between order and neglect, also in their own rooms. Teenagers often don't want us to even come close to their rooms, and we should also respect their wishes not to clean their rooms against their will. I found that my children rarely said no, when I offered to help them, but it was important to choose the right moment and the right tone. It's no use saying, 'What a pig-sty!' or 'I can't stand this chaos and filth any longer.' I usually said something like, 'I have some time tomorrow. If you feel like it, I can help you to do your room.' Or, 'If you want to tidy up a bit today, I can clean your room tomorrow.'

When my son turned thirteen, he greeted me with a great smile when I came back from work, telling me that he had given himself a special birthday present. I was surprised when he took me to his room and showed me that he had freshly made his bed, cleaned the windows, dusted everything, vacuumed and mopped the floor, and in a tiny vase he had put winter aconites from our garden. I was very grateful and profoundly moved because I knew that, come what may, deep within he loved beauty and order.

When he turned fourteen his room was such a catastrophe that I decided to offer him a nice clean bedroom for his birthday, as he had done for himself a year ago. He was very pleased and grateful. As it seemed to have been such a success, I decided that I would at least continue making his bed for him, but after three days he quite decidedly told me that he appreciated my birthday present but I should please leave his room alone now.

I am often asked what one could do to make a husband and the children participate more in the household chores. Well, I am neither an educator, nor a marriage counsellor, and there are no simple recipes.

Recently a mother told me that she had always expected the children to keep their bedrooms tidy and clean and that they had to help with other household chores. At some point she gave up because her children never wanted to do as they were told. Then, as soon as she stopped nagging, all the things she asked of them before were done of their own accord – quite simply because now it was no longer demanded of them. expected to do it. Her children are adults now, and recently confessed that they resented the continual pressure she put on them as children and had suffered because of her unreasonably high standards. This shows that order should serve, not rule our lives.

Women tend to have greater expectations of their families than men do. A woman hopes that her husband and children will sense that she needs help, or that their untidiness is causing her suffering, and that they will clear it without her asking. This is mostly wishful thinking! The result is frustration and disappointment. It is much easier and better to express a need, and then come to some agreement. The chores that need to be done can be discussed and then agreed on who is going to do what. Once there is an agreement, we can expect these things to be done. And if the arrangement does not work, we can address it again.

Our home not only offers protection against the elements, but is the space where we are able to be as we are, without having to pretend to be something else. Our efforts in creating an atmosphere that has a harmonious and healing influence on all who live there is something we can all strive for. And if to some extent we succeed in our endeavours, it is something that has a profound effect for the future, reaching far beyond the walls of our home.

10. Cleaning Schools with their Students

No matter whether schools are cleaned well or not, they vary greatly in how the classrooms are looked after. Some are beautiful, clean and tidy, while others are messy, with pictures hanging crookedly, shelves crammed with odds and ends, neglected plants gathering dust. Interestingly the behaviour of the pupils and students often reflects their surroundings.

In my opinion the cleanliness of schools is determined by the standards of the teachers. Where there is a good, harmonious school, the rooms are orderly and tidy. Sometimes, however, I see teachers' and meeting rooms in a mess, with overflowing bins, half-eaten apples, and dirty coffee cups. And then teachers wonder why they cannot resolve their conflicts and arrive at good decisions.

Often there are also places in schools where stuff simply collects, producing an image of disorder. Small storage rooms next to classrooms are sometimes full of things other than school supplies. All this has a deep effect on the pupils and students in the school, and shows itself in how they in turn care for their surroundings.

Student cleaning project

I have visited many different schools and training centres across Europe and America for many years. There is a wide range of quality standards and cleaning arrangements, ranging from professional cleaning services to small family businesses or volunteers. At many Waldorf schools parents do the cleaning; some schools are also cleaned with the help of students of higher grades.

There is a variety of reasons why schools invite me. They may want to save money. They want to scrutinise the existing services provided by the cleaning company, or they may not be satisfied with the quality of the cleaning services. Sometimes they are looking for a more environmentally friendly solution. At other times the motivation of the cleaning staff and/or parent body is weak, and they are seeking a new impetus. Or there may be a desire to tread new paths, for example, to clean the school together with some of its students.

In 2001 a school that my company was cleaning, needed to take urgent austerity measures. My suggestion was that students should be paid for cleaning their own school. I offered to induct them and provide support.

A list of services was already in existence, so the new plans were drawn up and all tasks divided among ten students. They were given a proper induction, and the quality of their work was checked weekly. This went well until someone took the view that the students now knew how to do the job, and the school could make greater savings by dispensing with my supervision, leaving the students to work completely independently. This did not last for long.

Generally the students knew exactly what to do, and were responsible and dependable, but they wanted to be supervised and guided. This is understandable because at that age their will power is not yet sufficiently developed to take everything upon themselves. To leave the whole co-ordination of personnel, planning, control, work schedules, checking and re-ordering of cleaning materials to young people is asking too much.

Since then I have introduced several projects where students clean their own school building. They establish their own cleaning company, specifically for their school. Experience shows that such a project depends entirely on the supervisor for its success or failure. However, there are distinct benefits to a school of such a project.

On an educational level:

* Students develop practical skills benefiting the real world.
* They develop new powers of perception in having to notice a range of details around the school building.
* Through physical activity their inertia and their time with computers or electronic gadgets is reduced.

- ❋ They learn of the importance of preserving valuable assets through the conscious care of their own school building.
- ❋ They are taught ecological and sustainable values through the practical cleaning their own school.
- ❋ A well cared for environment has a positive effect on the concentration and academic performance of students.

On a social level:

- ❋ Through the joint care of the school building, social skills are developed.
- ❋ Through deliberate care a new relationship to the school building is created, which can lead to a reduction in vandalism and violence. Violence and aggression are reduced if teachers and pupils feel equally responsible for their school.
- ❋ The experience of cleaning can lead to a change in attitudes toward cleaning and to people who clean.
- ❋ An understanding of economic and legal aspects is enhanced through the experience of running of a small business.

From concept to reality

Often the initial idea comes from the parent body who want a well cared-for school. A group of interested parents is formed and works until the project is able to be presented as an initiative to the responsible people in the school.

The there are the tasks. When I visit a school, I talk with teachers, students and parents to clarify the willingness and abilities of all parties. A decision has to be made about whether the students initially take on one part of the school building or all of it. Then a list of specifications has to be drawn up, the required number of students identified and costs calculated.

Possible objections

Often when a such project is presented and discussed various questions, problems or objections come up.

Initially additional costs may result. Existing inventory will often need to be replaced. More cleaning products and more material is required as many more students than the number of existing cleaning staff are employed, because the students can usually only manage a maximum of one or two hours per week. This also means more administrative work, as the coordination and planning takes time, and requires overview and patience.

Consulting costs are for setting up and training. I am often asked to induct the students at least once, but sometimes only the person who is to lead the group. This is often a miscalculation, as this person does not have the experience to accurately estimate how much time should be allocated for each task. Any initial savings are often more expensive in the long term. A school in Berlin agreed on a cleaning project with high school students even though the new project was slightly more expensive than the existing cleaning arrangement. The teaching staff appreciated the educational side of the project so much that they were prepared to bear the additional costs. This is commendable, but it highlights the necessity of looking at the finances very carefully. For example, if initially too much time is allocated for cleaning a classroom, it accumulates over the course of the year, considerably increasing the cost. The students should be inducted so well at the beginning that the work can be done in the allotted time. This requires an experienced person, or a supervisor who has been inducted very well. This takes time and money, but in my experience costs can then be reduced in the long term, if there is an adequate initial investment.

What is to happen with the personnel being laid off? This is really an important aspect. If it is a cleaning company it is usually possible for them to redeploy the personnel elsewhere. Sometimes notice is given because something is wrong with the quality (which for me is always a legitimate reason for terminating a contract). It is sometimes possible to integrate the some of the existing cleaning staff in the project.

Are young people open to some of the background I provide as motivation? I can only say, yes, they are open. A ninth-grader once asked me after a lecture in which I mentioned 'invisible' dirt, 'If there is unseen dirt, is there also an invisible ecology?' No adult has ever asked me this question.

Training

Following aspects should be covered when inducting students.

- *Perception:* Someone who does not notice what needs doing, will not clean well. Conscious observation always connects us with something. This connection in turn enables us to fully concentrate on the task – one might even say surrender ourselves to the task.
- *Method:* Where do I start, how do I handle the broom, and what is my posture like? How do I plan the work processes?
- *Rhythm:* How often and what tasks are performed? Who is working on what days? What are my movements and gestures like – are they rhythmic, harmonious, flowing, or hectic, tense, irritable? Practising movements is to be encouraged and supported.
- *Resources and materials:* What equipment and which cleaning materials do I use on which surface? How do I leave my tools when I finish my work – is everything clean, replenished and in order? Usually the next day it is someone else's turn, and it is important that they can begin working without delay in order to keep to the schedule.

The purpose of student cleaning

The purpose of such a project is not just to remove the dirt, but to help the development of young people and of the whole school community. Recognising the project's educational significance and the potential to change young people's attitude to work are for me the most important aspects.

Initially, of course, the incentive for the students is often their remuneration. The prospect of earning money is stronger than their instinctive aversion to cleaning. So I try from the first moment to imbue the students with the importance and dignity of their task. I talk with them about cleaning from the perspective of a cleaner. I tell them some of my experiences, for instance how in one school that I cleaned, a group of boys kept trying to provoke me verbally.

Their ring leader sometimes threw rubbish at my feet saying, 'Well, now you've got something to do.' Once, when he had just thrown some orange peel on the floor, I called him by his name. He was surprised and looked at me. I said, 'That surprises you, doesn't it? You do not know my name, but I know your name. And I know a lot more about you. The way you behave and the way you treat me, says a lot about you.' That was the last time that he behaved in this manner. Six months later he asked me if he could learn to clean with me during the summer holidays.

The activity of cleaning, together with a conscious perception of the environment, strengthens self-motivation and self-control. Young people learn to take responsibility for their actions, and this develops a strong will. Their will is further shaped and strengthened during the cleaning activity by their perception of the environment, their self-perception, as well as through rhythmic and deliberate movements. They will also learn that it rarely pays off to do something as quickly as possible.

Once students begin to care for their school building, radical changes occur. The buildings remain cleaner and vandalism is reduced drastically (this is particularly noticeable in the toilets). Classmates want to support their cleaning peers, and because there are so many of them, they point out to each other any causes of dirt or disorderliness. Occasionally the students even educate the teachers.

The school as a living organism

Just as our own home can be experienced as an organism (Chapter 3), so too can a school building be seen as a living organism. Every organism thrives on care that is bestowed upon it. By caring of a school building young people learn about conscious, deliberate action and forming a relationship with things in their care. That is something that is of value for their whole lifetime.

Schools are vital social institutions for the future of society. It is here that young people learn social behaviour every day, creating relationships to other people as well as to their physical environment. Initially a relationship is formed through the senses, and so a training of the senses helps to builds a healthy relationship with the world. Conscious caring is nurtures a relationship. We cannot consciously and lovingly deal with anything or anyone without having some kind of a relationship. Such a relationship reduces the propensity towards violence, because most people do not want to destroy that with which they have established a positive relationship.

Violence is a social issue, not a youth problem. We find vandalism everywhere, but mostly in places that have already been neglected. In their book about school violence, Gisela and Axel Preuschoff write following.

> Violent tendencies and aggression can be reduced if teachers and students together feel responsible for their school, because they have a say in organising their school. Frustration and experiences of failure of all kind must be avoided. The school must not degenerate into a knowledge factory, but must take its educational task seriously.[1]

After a week working with students at the Institute for Waldorf Education in Witten Annen, Germany, I received the following letter from a Brazilian student.

> On the third day of the big cleaning job after the new building was completed, I was completely shattered. The work was not too difficult, and I did not know why I was so tired. I could not restrain myself cried out, 'I hate cleaning.'
> My aggressive words were countered by a loving response, 'Cleaning is very important in the world. You have to love cleaning.'
> Following the construction there was to be six weeks

of cleaning. Every morning I tried to understand, why I did not like cleaning. I remembered the vultures at Santos beach, they ate everything the sea washed up on the beach. Nobody needs to tell the vultures how to clean: they do it instinctively. But people need to learn to clean; not only that, they need to learn to love cleaning. Then the question arose, can people learn to love?

Every morning a long stairway and a hall wait to be cleaned. I know every step and every corner of my designated area. I know exactly where the dust gathers. I also know that there is a beautiful sculpture with a lot of dark dust underneath. The beautiful sculpture pardons the dirt. Everyone sees the beauty of the sculpture, but I see only dirt. I cannot forgive myself for leaving the dirt. I know it is there.

Then I understood why I was so tired: I could not stand my own filthiness.

For a week I have been trying to calmly ignore the sculpture. Finally I tackled it with water and soap. Then I put back the sculpture. All is done. Now I can appreciate its beauty. I no longer see only the dirt. The institute is really beautiful, but my hall has something special for me.
In six weeks I did not learn to love cleaning, but I began to realise that I can learn to love spaces.

Preventing neglect

The opposite of care is neglect. Neglect is something insidious: it begins in all the corners we do not penetrate with cleaning or our awareness. It spreads when damaged property is not repaired, and when dirt and waste are not removed immediately. Neglect is a passive form of vandalism, creating an environment for violence and destruction.

Following a workshop with the teaching staff of a school, a major operation by nearly all the teachers liberated the staff room of much accumulated debris and layers of dust. Stuff that had collected here was sorted and disposed of. The state of the room had poisoned the social atmosphere and work ethic. I observed how long-standing, serious conflicts disappeared as if by magic, triggered by this thorough cleaning of the staff room.

Having to teach in neglected classrooms or organise teachers' meetings in a chaotic uncared-for staff room has nothing to do with education. Creating healthy connections between people, spaces and functions is practical schooling for life.

I sincerely hope that we learn the value of cleaning. Cleaning, especially if it is done together with others, is an important social practice and creates a foundation for a harmonious life.

Questions and answers

What can you know about a school when you see its state?
I can only describe my impressions and the images that arise within in me. For example, I visited a school and then was asked for my impression. I instinctively replied, 'The insight into the basics and overview are lacking.'

My assessment was apt, but people wanted to know how I could describe the condition so succinctly. Walking through the school I had noticed the very neglected, tired-looking floor. This was a sure sign that there was no awareness of the basis or foundation on which they walked. All the windows in the doors of the corridors were very dirty just at eye level. A clear view was impossible.

Did you have other impressions you can describe?
If things are lying around where they obviously don't belong, or if there is unfinished work, I'm tempted to think there is indecisiveness among the teachers which could also indicate difficulties in communication. Lack of structure can often be deduced from the state of the staff room or meeting rooms.

You are often in schools. Are there large differences in standards of care?
Yes, there are very big differences. Sometimes I feel the teachers are overburdened, resulting in an escape into 'not noticing'. The school was beautifully built, but exhausted everyone in the process. Nowadays

there is often facility management during the planning phase. People with experience in maintenance and cleaning are consulted. If the design is not practical, maintenance and cleaning costs will be unnecessarily high after completion.

In the pioneering stage of a school people are often over-with their time. When this phase is over and the founding members have gone, the new staff do not know how it once was. A kind of emptiness arises; classrooms and staff rooms are stuffed full of things, causing chaos. I am often invited at that stage because a change is wanted.

Sometimes, the people arranging and assigning cleaning tasks simply do not know what is entailed. A large school employed two women who worked six hours a day. I was invited because it was not clean. I was indignant, as six hours was not even sufficient for the sanitary facilities. In another school, a cleaning company was contracted for fifteen hours a day. For this school twenty-five hours per week would have been perfectly adequate. Ignorance on the part of those organising the cleaning is no excuse. In each case a professional could have been asked, or more than one tender for the job could have been obtained.

You advise different institutions on cleaning their premises. Is cleaning actually a communal task, and does the way it is handled have an effect on the community?
I try to meet the needs of my clients. When I propose a cleaning arrangement, I also offer to give the necessary instructions. As far as possible, I support the idea that high school students, for example, clean their school building themselves. I prefer to take on the instruction of the students myself. Experience shows that students who clean their own school, connect in a different way with it.

I strongly support things that can be arranged communally. There is always the danger of certain people not being willing to commit. Some parents who have to clean a kindergarten do not have a particularly great desire to do the work and consequently the cleaning is superficial. Some kindergarten teachers recommend that parents who like cleaning receive a fee, and those who do not like cleaning are not obliged to do it. A room that is cleaned unwillingly has a different atmosphere.

11. Practicalities

Where do I start?

Getting organised and cleaning

When my children were young, I spent 15 minutes early in the mornings bringing order into our home. At bedtime, I planned what I would do in those 15 minutes the next morning, and was thus able to use the time effectively. These early morning acts of will brought a sense of purpose to the day, and proved to be a success.

Before going to bed, it can be a help to create an image of how we want to shape the following day. Of course, it often turns out quite differently from what we had intended, but this preparation in the evenings nonetheless offers a support.

Before actually starting with the cleaning or tidying up, just stand in the doorway and look at the room you want to tackle. Perceive it as one whole and then ask yourself, what is bothering you most in this room? Often it is what we kept put off doing for whatever reason. Begin with the most bothersome task. Sometimes it seems as if this thing has taken on a life of its own, and that is why you don't want to look at it anymore. Once you have started at this point, blocked up energy is released. Once you have tackled this very difficult corner, you seem to find the strength to continue

Start with the room which irritates you most

1. Try to find out what bothers you most in this room and set to work there.
2. Stand in the doorway for a moment, look at the space; direct your gaze right around the room from the left (or the right, it does not matter) and from top to bottom. Then look at everything in the middle of the room, and then finally look at the floor.
3. If what bothers you most is going to be a major operation (for example, sorting out the photographs), think carefully if you should not first tackle other things that are more urgent (like paying invoices or filing important papers). If you are determined to sort out the photographs, prepare everything in detail beforehand. You will need a large table, several albums, things for sticking and labelling, and don't forget a large waste paper basket.
4. Plan large-scale operations separately from the actual clean-up; otherwise you will not make progress.

The cleaning process

Essentials

- ❉ *Perception:* What is not noticed is not cleaned.
- ❉ *Structure:* What and how much do I want to do?
- ❉ *System:* Where do I start and how do I go about it (from top to bottom, etc.)?
- ❉ *Planning a rhythm:* How often, on what day do I clean?
- ❉ *Rhythm in our actions:* What movements and gestures do I use when cleaning – frantic, hurried movements, or deliberate harmonious ones? Observe your body and how I handle and take care of something.
- ❉ *Method:* Perception is the key word here. How do I use my gestures? When am I working with my whole body and arms,

and when do I use my fingertips? You can't clean a corner with large gestures of your arm. Only by using your fingertips will the corner be cleaned and penetrated. (It is striking how often cooking pots are cleaned well on the inside, but not so well on the outside; with their lids the opposite seems to be the case.)

Clearing space before beginning

Most accidents happen at home, so we should try to avoid pitfalls as prevention saves us time and nerves. A simple rule is, when tidying, always start with the floor. That way we not only live less dangerously, but the cleared space immediately (at least) gives an impression of order.

Disorder is often caused because too much has been accumulated, the living spaces are poorly organised, or simply because not enough space is available. To maintain a solid level of order is a great help, especially if there are children in the house. This is not easy, but with practice it avoids periodic big clean-ups. Start practising sooner rather than later and, if possible, with the whole family.

Clearing up primarily means that we check at regular brief intervals, whether we really need the things that take up space. Anything that has not been used during the last six months can go into a storeroom, cellar or loft. If something has not been used for more than a year, we should ask, does it deserve the space it takes up?

Creating a good system is part of creating order. If everything that is needed in our home has its place, our children will soon learn that nothing else should go there.

Different rooms in the home

The kitchen

The daily clearing of the kitchen makes life easier. Already at breakfast, we can determine the course of the day.

❋ Don't leave the table empty-handed.

❋ Return everything, including jam, butter, milk to its place immediately after use.

❋ Put dirty dishes straight into the dishwasher, wash them immediately.

Where things are kept in the kitchen should serve practical needs. How close are things to hand when I cook or bake? Too much running to and fro in the kitchen creates disorder. Arrange everything so that it can be put away quickly, without having to move something else first. So don't pile things up in cupboards: it makes returning things difficult, and having to rummage in a cupboard before putting something away is cumbersome.

It helps keeping things tidy if only a few items are on the working surfaces. Keep wooden spoons by the stove, and salt, common herbs and spices close by.

Before cooking or baking, first make space. Empty the dishwasher and wash up anything left around, so you can clean up easily as you work. Put utensils into the dishwasher or wash them up immediately. As soon as flour, butter and eggs are no longer needed, put them back where they belong. In this way chaos will never arise.

Create order in the refrigerator before shopping. Check availability and condition of fresh fruits and vegetables. From time to time check the order in the freezer and the shelf life of food.

Refrigerator interior: Clean the inside well with baking soda, as it scours without scratching and also acts as disinfectant. A little baking soda on a small plate also helps to absorb odour (like onion or cheese).

Unidentified odour in refrigerator: Check bottle racks in the door. Milk or cream quickly cause odour if they are accidentally spilled.

Stove and Oven: Spray burnt areas with soda and remove with a scraper. To remove remaining dirt, spray the sides and the grid with soda and remove with steel wool. Do not use steel wool in self-cleaning ovens. Wipe with a damp cloth.

Air vent: This is easy to clean with a fibre cloth and soda.

Dishwasher: The polished chrome steel door can be cleaned very well with water and fibre cloth. The inner edges of the door should be sprayed and wiped from time to time with soda, so they do not form a hard crust. If cleaned regularly a fibre cloth and water will suffice.

Floor: Sweep the floor daily and mop when needed.

Regular tasks: Since kitchen surfaces tend to greasy, it helps to wipe the all surfaces and containers down regularly, with a damp fibre cloth. At least every six months wipe down cabinets, as well as their top surfaces and any containers on them.

Waste and compost bucket: Every time we empty the bin or compost bucket wipe or scrub the cabinet in which they are kept. Sometimes bits drop down beside the containers and vermin may be attracted if it is not cleaned regularly.

Moths: To prevent infiltration of flour moths keep foods such as flour, ground nuts, herbal teas and dried fruits in tightly closed containers. Regularly check your bread bin and the toaster. They love breadcrumbs.

Bathrooms

We can avoid disorder the bathroom by clearing away toothpaste, deodorant, shaving foam, etc. immediately after use.

In hard water areas everyone should dry tiles and surfaces in bath or shower with a squeegee directly after showering or bathing to avoid calcium deposits.

Remove hair after each use. don't wash it away as it will clog the drains.

Before wet areas are cleaned, first sweep or vacuum the floor so that no hair or dust residue sticks to the floor. They can then be mopped.

Clean the overflow in the sink regularly with a brush to prevent mould forming and the related odour.

Do not use abrasive cleaners, but a slightly acidic medium, for example citric acid. Abrasive cleaners damage the ceramic surfaces and need a lot of rinsing to avoid deposits.

To remove heavy limescale from tiles, spray them well with the showerhead so that the grouting is saturated with water. If you then use a slightly stronger cleaning agent, such as citric acid or cleaning vinegar, the grouting will not be dissolved by the acid.

Mould in the bathroom or in the grouting is cleaned best of all with the right gestures. Clean the grouting with a fibre cloth using your finger tips. If the mould is too far advanced, take a little chlorine bleach (1 teaspoon to about $\frac{1}{4}$ litre/quart water) to clean, then rinse and dry well. Once cleaned, treat grouting with tea tree oil or grapefruit seed oil, to prevent further growth. I use a small paintbrush to do this. Mould in silicone grouting remains because the mould forms below the surface. Once it turns black it should be replaced.

After washing shower curtains, immerse and soak them in salt water. This prevents mould growing. If treated regularly the curtains will remain nice.

Regularly check the mirror cabinet above the sink. Remove and discard old medicines. Check for residue under cosmetics bottles, or the shelves will become very sticky. Dust the surfaces twice a month, because dust forms quickly due to the heat of the lights.

Living room, dining room, bedrooms

Children's' bedrooms (especially while the children are young) should be kept tidy and cleaned regularly. Before starting make sure the toys are stored in baskets or containers (again it is easier if everything has its proper place). Before going to bed, children can be encouraged to create order with help from their parents. Instead of leaving clothes carelessly on the floor, look at them, and decide together whether they should go into the laundry basket or be laid out to be worn again the next day. I never told a bedtime story in a messy room.

Before birthdays, Christmas or Easter is a good time to clear out the rooms. In our family we used to sort out toys to make room for new things. We would put all the toys that were still played with back in their places. For the rest we had three containers: one for broken or unwanted toys that could be thrown away, one for the toys that would be sent to the children in Africa, and one for the toys that would be stored for the time being. When these were then taken out again after some time there was great rejoicing. Usually at the next tidy-up these things were allowed to go to Africa.

For your own bedroom, I would suggest if possible, not to have a desk or working area where you risk leaving unfinished business overnight. Avoid having an armchair if it only serves as a dumping place for clothes. It is good to be surrounded by beauty and order while we rest. Check from time to time to see what is kept under your bed and on top of your cupboards.

All rooms

- Remove cobwebs regularly, find hidden dust traps and thoroughly remove all dust, even behind the furniture and pictures.
- Make sure there is enough space for shoes, as this often creates disorder in the hallway.
- Avoid hanging coats on or behind doors.
- Dust radiators at least twice a year (for instance, before and after the heating period). We often assume that we get colds and flu when the weather turns cold, but it is often because some of last year's viruses survived in the dust. Once the heating is turned on, the heat makes the dust rise and this makes us ill.
- Old newspapers, magazines and catalogues don't belong in the living room.
- Check every evening before bedtime that all personal items have been removed from common spaces. If everyone picks up their own stuff, things will basically be tidy.
- Table linen is best stored near the dining table.
- Bed linen is best stored in the bedroom, towels in the bathroom.

Odds and ends

Paperwork

Order in all personal records should be created as regularly as possible. Even when opening the mail, I try to sort it all. Catalogues and advertising mail, which I do not need, go directly into the recycling bin, as do the envelopes of the opened letters. Don't keep all the old envelopes as notepaper by the phone!

It can be helpful to keep different trays or drawers for different things (see 'Lifestyle habits' in Chapter 8). These can then be dealt with regularly and then filed, so the trays are empty again.

Tidying made easy

Wardrobe: To have a good overview of your wardrobe, find a good system for organising it. Starting with a good clear always helps (see 'Clothing' in Chapter 8 for more). For instance, use a dresser for woollens, with drawers for sweaters, gloves, hats and scarves. In the wardrobe hang smart things that are not worn very often to one side, followed by coats and jackets, and on the other side hang everyday clothes, starting with blouses, then skirts and then trousers. Put T-shirts and track suits at eye level, so you can see them. Underwear, stockings, socks and pyjamas, can be in separate drawers.

Care of cleaning equipment: Look after cleaning equipment and materials. All cleaning agents and equipment should always be returned to where they were found. Replenish cleaning agents immediately after use. This helps getting started the next day. All sponges, fibre cloths and floor cloths should be rinsed clean after use and hung to dry. The vacuum cleaner should be checked regularly so that the bag is not too full; filters have to be changed. Before putting away the vacuum cleaner, check whether the cleaning cupboard needs vacuuming.

Basement, attic and storage rooms: It is good to go through from time to time to remove cobwebs and to vacuum, in order to permeate the room. Hanging a bunch of dried sage leaves somewhere and replacing it with the change of seasons helps create a rhythm in you're the care of these spaces.

If you are planning a major clean-up operation in your house, start with the storage areas. There are usually things that haven't been used for a long time and may not needed. Once free space is created here, it is easier to put away the things that clutter up the common spaces in the home.

Laundry room: Dust and humidity rapidly accumulate here. Vacuum and air the room frequently, and remove cobwebs to discourage permanent guests. Once a year, the pipes and other items (such as the hot water boiler) could be dusted thoroughly.

Look after your washing machine by wiping it after use. At least once a month take out and clean the detergent drawer as calcium deposits and mould may build us. Clean filters regularly.

Tips and tricks

- ※ Chewing gum can be removed with ice or frost spray. Remove solid or crumbly particles immediately. On clothing, machine wash together with an old microfibre cloth.
- ※ Scratches on wood can be partially removed with a cork dipped in a vinegar-oil mixture. Rub scratches in a circular motion; repeat the process several times.
- ※ Patent leather shoes with stains: Rub the affected area thoroughly with half an onion. Wipe afterwards with a cloth.
- ※ Wash soft leather gloves in soapy water, adding a few drops of olive oil to the last rinse.
- ※ Rubber gloves: Sprinkle the inside with a little cornstarch or talc. It makes them easier put on and take off.

Bugs and infestations

Moths: Moths and the larvae of carpet beetles and fur beetles can cause great damage to textiles. For prevention use little bags of cedarwood, curd soap, lavender or cloves, or use neem oil. Moths have nothing to do with hygiene or disorder. Moths are on the increase, because clothing made of natural fibres has become more popular again. Those who have only clothes made from artificial fibres in their wardrobe need not fear these little creatures. They prefer pure wool, especially cashmere. Empty the wardrobe and inspect the contents about every six months. Wash the wardrobe with vinegar or rosemary oil, especially the corners, and then ventilate it well and let it dry. Only then should clothes be reorganised.

Once you have an infestation of clothes moths, carpet beetles or fur beetle larvae, this is not enough. Wash clothing that has been infested at 60°C (140°F). Where clothing cannot be washed at such a high temperature use a neem oil insecticide. This kills the larvae of clothes moths, carpet beetles and fur beetles within a few days. The effect of this food poison lasts for several months.

Ants: Sprinkle chalk or baby powder (both contain talcum powder) across the spot where ants are entering your house. More Frequent applications are better than spreading one thick layer. Repeat treatment after rainy weather.

To prevent fleas use clove oil diluted in water or alcohol and spray carpets and beds.

Invasions of pests such as silverfish, dust lice, lice, cockroaches and fleas can be treated with a diatomaceous earth insecticide (such as Insecto-Sec) which slits open the skin of the insects, and causes them to dehydrate. This insecticide has a purely physical action and can therefore be readily used in kitchen cupboards. Spread it where the insects are in corners and crevices. Treated surface must remain dry. Repeat as necessary. If cats avoid their treated sleeping place, cover it with a fine cloth.

Cleaning agents and tools

Environmental considerations

In general, people have become more environmentally conscious. Yet there is still a lack of commitment regarding ecological or organic cleaning agents and even more so regarding ecological cosmetics. People are generally not well informed and often lack sufficient patience to let them work. Many still believe that environmentally friendly cleaning products are more expensive and less effective, but this is no longer the case.

Nowadays so much information is available about cleaning products and their ingredients that there really is no excuse for responsible adults to use harmful cleaning agents or cosmetics.

The most generally used cleaning agents are acids, alkalines, neutral agents, abrasives and dissolving agents. Glass scrapers and microfibres are useful tools.

Acids

Citric, lactic, formic and vinegar (avoid sulphuric, hydrochloric and phosphoric acids and salts).

Use in bathrooms, showers, toilets, basins, kitchen sinks, etc., as well as on glass, porcelain, and vases. For general cleaning, spray and then wipe with good fibre cloth; no rinsing needed. Regular use prevents limescale deposits. Also use to remove cement traces on floors or other surfaces after building work. Dilute acid well before using on chrome and metal, or it may cause stains.

Use as a neutralising agent after treating fabrics or carpets with alkaline products or soap. Rinse with water to which a dash of lemon juice or vinegar has been added, to prevent the fibres from becoming brittle.

Acidic stains, such as a vomit or fruit, should be treating with acid, such as a little lemon juice, perhaps even yoghurt or the slightly acidic extract of the Panama tree, to avoid staining.

If using a bathroom cleaner such as Ecover or Sonett with a microfibre cloth, it is quite enough to use it as a 1:10 dilution.

Never use acid on marble, granite or other stone surfaces which are not acid resistant.

Alkalines

Crystal soda (also called washing soda or soda crystals), bicarbonate of soda (baking soda), liquid soap and gall soap. Avoid ammoniac and ammonium chloride.

Use to remove grease from kitchen tiles, ovens and aeration vents. Good for stain removal, but do not to use on acidic fruit stains as they will only discolour. Excellent for thorough cleaning, but be careful to check first when using on painted surfaces as it may bleach. Soda removes old layers of dirt and polish from floors.

Never use on surfaces containing natural oils such as linoleum or oiled wood, as it breaks down fat and oil particles, causing brittleness.

Neutral agents

All purpose cleaners (which includes water!) can be used on all surfaces where no specific care is required, such as synthetic surfaces (Formica) or painted surfaces. It is not suitable for wet areas in hard water regions as it does not remove limescale.

Abrasives

Marble paste, quartz, pumice, ash, Viennese chalk. Avoid scouring cream or powder.

Use abrasives very sparingly and only in the right areas. It is very good to remove scratches and black marks caused by pots and pans, cutlery, keys, or pencils. Use on badly burnt surfaces with a scouring pad. Can be used on stoves and in fridges to remove grey or yellow lines. Avoid using it in bathrooms, basins, etc. as it can scratch surfaces. Enamel bathtubs will lose their coating after repeated use.

Rinse very well after use, as abrasives may leave deposits which could even block pipes if used excessively.

Dissolving agents

Alcohol, turpentine, benzene, petrol, paraffin (kerosene), citrus (orange) oil.

Only use when specifically needed, as surfaces may be damaged. Try to remove glue residues from tape, carpets or stickers with the glass scraper or microfibre first. If this does not work, use lamp oil (paraffin).

Glass scraper

Produced by Unger, the Trim 10+1 glass scraper is a professional double-edged blade made from tempered Swedish steel for cleaning glass. It can be hand-held or attached to a telescopic handle. I find it very useful for removing adhesive tape, paint spots and even insect marks on windows, as well as burnt encrustation from ovens and especially from glass oven doors. I have also used it to remove limescale build-up from flat surfaces, layers of old grease, chewing gum, dirt build-up on old floors and so on. By removing resistant dirt manually, you can often avoid using dissolving agents.

Microfibres

They can be used on virtually all surfaces and mostly without cleaning agents and an absolute minimum of water. However, take care when using on oiled or polished surfaces, because it can remove oil (unless produced specifically for oiled surfaces). They are excellent for removing stains from fabric and carpets. Invest in good quality fibres that are recyclable, such as Enjo, and follow instructions carefully.

Day-to-day cleaning

After years of experience I have been able to reduce the cleaning products I regularly use to three. In addition I use dishwashing liquid and washing powders or liquids.

1. *Citric acid* for bathroom cleaning and lime scale removal. Lemons, oranges, limes, and other citrus fruits contain high concentrations of citric acid.

    Dilute 2 teaspoons of citric acid in 500ml of water in a spray bottle for general cleaning in bathrooms and toilets. For decalcifying it could be more concentrated.
2. *Soda crystals* for greasy surfaces. Sodium carbonate (also known as washing soda, soda ash, or sal soda) effectively removes oil, grease, and alcohol stains. It is also used as a descaling agent in coffee pots, espresso machines, etc. It is a water softener during laundry, reducing the amount of detergent needed.

    Dilute 2 tablespoons of crystal soda in 500 ml (½ quart) water in a spray bottle for general use. Make sure to wipe down well.
3. *Water* for all other surfaces and uses. Can water be used as a detergent? I have been experimenting with some specially prepared cleaning waters for years now, with outstanding results.

Cleaning waters

There are various methods of treating water for cleaning.
Butzwasser is produced using a process of deisolysis by the Munich Light Matrix Laboratory (more information *www.lichtmatrix.de/en*). Use 7 drops of *Butzwasser* on 1 litre (quart) of tap water for all surfaces, mirrors, windows, floors.

AquaVeda is produced by energising the water (a little more information *www.aqua-veda.de* in German only). Use 6 drops on 1 litre (quart) of water for cleaning. AquaVeda also make a product for laundry, adding 24 drops to a load of washing.

Toucan-Eco is ionised water which contains a special cell in the spray and jug which uses electrochemical activation to convert the salt and water into an activated solution with disinfectant and detergent properties (more on this British company at *www.toucan-eco.com*).*

The activated fluid is simple and inexpensive to produce, using ordinary tap water, a small amount of salt, and a minute amount of electricity. Just pour tap water into the spray dispenser or jug, add 2 g ($^1/_3$ tsp) of salt, activate on the base station for 3 minutes and the combined activated cleaner/disinfectant is ready to use.

Bawell water ionisers are made in Florida. The company has been advocating the uses of alkaline ionised water for over ten years primarily for health reasons (for more see www.bawellwaterionizers.com).

Bawell quote research from Penn State University states:

> Water that is electrolyzed can be used to replace toxic chemicals for cleaning and disinfecting. Scientific reports published on PubMed show fruits, vegetables, and even meat can be cleaned with electrolyzed, ionised water to remove and neutralise dirt, bacteria, toxic pesticides and chemicals.[1]

Another ionised water system is produced by Healing Water Machines in California (www.HealingWaterMachines.com).

People sensitive to chemicals are enthused about the cleaning ability of ionised water, which can be made at home from your own faucet tap.

This new water isn't new, but it is becoming more popular because people are increasingly concerned with green issues.

Disinfection

It is becoming increasingly difficult to decide freely, which means to use for cleaning and disinfecting community flats, old people's homes, nursing homes, as well as homes in social therapeutic settings. Regulations and controls on hygiene and disinfection are becoming more stringent, and often confuse staff. I would suggest finding out more about ionised water, which is becoming better known and increasingly used in hospitals in Asia and Europe.

Sonett is a company that offers a good alternative to conventional disinfectant products. Their Multi Surface and Glass Cleaner is a herbal disinfectant with a wide range of applications in homes, schools, clinics, and food processing companies.* It is a ready solution that can be applied by spraying or wiping.

There are also antiseptic antibacterial essential oils such as thyme, lavender, rosemary, peppermint, lemon eucalyptus, eucalyptus, tea tree and rose.

Fragrances

The use of synthetic fragrances has grown tremendously over the last few years. They are in every taxi, hotel room and many other places.

Beware of so-called chemically 'identical' fragrances, they are not really identical. In view of the increasing number of sensitive people, the transparency of future ingredient declarations is to be commended in each case. The new EU laws, however, treat natural fragrances and essential oil components in the same way as synthetically produced fragrances and thus completely distort reality.

Pure essential oils occur in nature, during the course of the year, in the rhythm of day and night. The light of the sun, the warmth of the ground, determine what they store in them. The essential oil is the essence of the plant, and often contains more than 100 different components that complement and enhance each other.

Synthetic fragrances are largely derived from petroleum or, and attempt to emulate natural scents. However, they do this only in a narrow sense, and are far removed from the living totality of fragrant plants. Plants produce pure essential oils in the rhythm of day and night and of the year. The light of the sun, the warmth of the ground and many other factors determine their composition. Essential oils often contain more than a hundred different components. that

* The disinfectant is tested to EN 1276 and conforms to European biocides directives.

complement and enhance each other. By contrast, the many different components of synthetic fragrances are chemical residues which are often allergens.

Studies comparing natural essential oils with similar synthetic fragrances have shown marked difference in reactions of allergic people. Natural essential oils produced no or only limited reactions. In aromatherapy, too, the greatly superior efficacy of pure essential oils is well known.[2] Pure natural aromatic fragrances have a harmonising and therapeutic effect, whereas synthetically produced fragrances are mere mockeries which also pollute the air.

Environmentally friendly tips for your home

Being environmentally friendly is not only a matter of using the right cleaning agents, but also of respecting ecological, economic and social aspects in the caring and upkeep of buildings.

- ❊ Use as little water as possible.
- ❊ Every time you clean, use the correct dosage of suitable products. Both your cleaning products and equipment should be suitable for the task and used correctly.
- ❊ Discard unnecessary products, but make sure that there are suitable products for the care of different surfaces and areas.
- ❊ As far as possible use mechanical or manual procedures instead of chemical cleaning agents for the removal of old layers of dirt.
- ❊ Adapt the amount of cleaning and caring to need and usage. By developing an awareness of what is needed, the work can be planned flexibly.
- ❊ Deep (spring) cleaning should be planned according to

* According to European standards EN 1276, EN 1650, EN 13697 it is effective against bacteria, yeasts and fungi. According to vaccinia virus and BVDV-certificate report of November 4, 2009 effective against all enveloped viruses (claim 'limited virucidal activity'). This includes activity against HBV, HCV, HIV, herpes simplex, and all human and animal influenza viruses including H5N1, H1N1. According to the European standard EN 14476, 2007-02, it is effective against norovirus.

need and time available, not to a strict schedule, yet it
should not be neglected.

※ Maintaining the value of our homes and the objects we
live with is an important aim if we want to clean in an
environmentally-friendly way.

※ Defects (dripping faucets/taps, broken plugs), broken
objects, leaks, or traces of pests (rodents, moths, ants, etc.)
should be followed up immediately, to prevent further
damage.

※ Replace broken light bulbs.

※ Note any damage caused while cleaning, (like denting
walls or furniture, spilling water or blowing fuses) If you
can't repair it yourself, get it seen to.

※ Try to use products in refillable or recyclable containers.
The bigger the container, the cheaper it will be. Try to
use locally produced products. Transporting goods long
distances is not very green.

Nobody can do everything, but everyone can do something. Even
without money we can make a contribution towards the environment.
protection, nature conservation and to protection of species. Even very
Small changes in our everyday life will benefit the environment and
have a direct impact on global climate.

Our consumables

※ Pay attention to packaging. Returnable bottles avoid waste
piles. PVC packaging contains carcinogenic substances,
which can escape into the environment. Great amounts of
energy are used to produce aluminium cans.

※ When buying furniture pay attention to the wood. Make
sure it comes from sustainable forestry (FSC certified).

※ Save electricity. Even the most environmentally friendly
energy production requires intervention in nature.

※ When shopping for food, try to buy local products. Low
food miles also provide better quality food.

✳ Make do without eating 'exotic' delicacies.
✳ Go for locally produced fish and make sure that it is sustainable (MSC certified).

Nature and the garden

✳ Discover the diversity of plants and animals on your Sunday walk, without disturbing them.
✳ Do not take wild animals home with you, unless they are demonstrably injured or orphaned. Leave rare plants in nature.
✳ Do not throw rubbish away carelessly; dispose of it properly. A healthy environment is the foundation for the survival of all species.
✳ Give a piece of garden as a gift to nature. Ponds attract frogs and newts. Unmown meadows are a paradise for butterflies and other insects.
✳ Provide help for nesting and hibernating – nesting boxes for birds, bee boxes for wild bees, piles of leaves for hedgehogs.
✳ Do not use artificial fertilisers and pesticides.
✳ Plant native trees and shrubs. Their fruits are food for songbirds.

There is much to discover, once we change our attitude towards cleaning, the environment and nature. There are always new situations and we are constantly challenged to find new solutions.

Laundry

The quality and cost of environmentally friendly detergents is no longer an excuse for not using them. We can do our bit for the environment by choosing a suitable detergent. A little research is needed, as not everything labelled 'organic' or 'natural' is in fact environmentally friendly. Some contain synthetic fragrances, some bio detergents have genetically modified enzymes.

Some companies are genuinely devoted to sustainability, for instance Sonett or Ecover, mentioned earlier. Sonett (www.sonett.com) is a company who is very sincerely and consequently devoted to sustainability. Their ingredients are completely biodegradable and free of allergens, phosphates or optical brighteners, using primarily herbal and mineral raw materials.

Check out whether the company has independent certification (like Ecogarantie in Europe), and whether they list all their ingredients (important for allergy sufferers).

Stain Removal

The best treatment for resistant stains is soaking

One of the greatest discoveries I have made was the use of effective micro-organisms (EM) to remove organic stains, even on the most precious and delicate fabrics. I have soaked a silk scarf – stained with rotten pumpkin – for three days and it came out perfectly. EM is a combination of useful naturally-existing micro-organisms that are not manipulated in any way. It comes in a liquid form and is widely available (search for 'effective micro-organisms' on the internet if necessary).

Some solutions given below are not totally environmentally-friendly and should only be used if you really want to save the stained article. This is because you often have to treat chemicals in a chemical way. My thanks to L.A. and H.A. Campbell for the arrangement and some of the suggestions in this section.[3]

Acids: Act quickly so that acid cannot damage the cloth. Sprinkle the stain with baking soda, dampen with water and allow to stand till bubbling stops. Rinse well in warm water. Alternatively, in a well-ventilated space hold the dampened stain over an open bottle of household ammonia so that the fumes can neutralise the acid. Rinse well. Most fruit, coffee & cola stains can be removed with Panama tree extract.

Adhesives: See Glues, gums & cellulose adhesives.

Adhesive tape: Dampen the dry fabric stain with cleaning water (see p. 210) and remove with a good fibre cloth.

Alcohol: Always treat these as soon as possible. Often stains are almost colourless at first, but turn brown on standing, washing and ironing. Fresh stains can be removed by sponging several times with warm water. If there is any mark left, pour glycerine on the dampened stain, rub lightly between the hands and leave for half an hour. Rinse in warm water.

Alkalis such as washing soda and ammonia, or cuticle remover, may destroy colour and rot material. Rinse at once in equal quantities of vinegar and water. Rinse well in warm water. If colour has been affected this cannot be corrected.

Baby oil: Rub some dishwashing liquid into the stain, leave for 10–15 minutes, then hot wash (60–65°C, 140–150°F) using your normal laundry detergent. If any stain remains, repeat the process. For non washable fabrics or articles, see Butter.

Berry stains: Dip stains into sour milk or natural yoghurt. Allow to sit for a while and then wash normally. Old stains can be soaked in EM.

Black tea: Soak in milk, then wash.

Bleach: Treat immediately with copious amounts of cold water. For chlorine bleach, add 1 tbsp vinegar in each 600 ml (½ quart) water. If the colour has been removed by the bleach, it cannot readily be restored, but try holding in fumes from an open bottle of ammonia in a well-ventilated space.

Blood: If fresh, sponge with cool salted water (1 tsp in 600 ml, ½ quart water) and rinse with clear water.

Old bloodstains on clothes: Soak overnight in water with gall soap and then wash as usual. Should the stain persist, soak in a EM for a longer period. Or you can try any of the following suggestions (they are in no particular order).

- ❋ Dilute hydrogen peroxide (1 part to 9 parts water). Purchase the strongest solution available from a pharmacy (usually 20 vol). Rinse well.
- ❋ Sponge with a 10% solution of oxalic acid, warmed to about 45°C (110°F). Rinse well.
- ❋ Sponge with dilute ammonia (1 tsp to 600 ml, ½ quart water). Rinse well.
- ❋ For thick or non-washable articles, e.g. mattresses, carpets, sprinkle with pepsin powder (from your pharmacy), or spread with a thick paste of raw starch and water, leave to dry, then brush off. Repeat if necessary.

Boot Polish: Sponge with a laundry pre-soak (spot stain remover) or with dry-cleaning fluid.

Candle wax and chewing gum can be effectively removed by putting what has been stained into the freezer until the wax or gum is hard and brittle, then it can be literally shattered off the object that has been stained. If there is a residue place the stain between clean, white blotters and press with a warm iron, changing the blotter as it becomes soiled. Then treat with gall soap. In the case of coloured wax there may still be a colour stain. Sponge with a liquid made by mixing equal parts of methylated spirits (denatured alcohol) and water.

Chewing gum: Scrape away as much as possible first. Rubbing the stain with ice will harden the gum and make this easier, especially on rugs and other heavy materials. For more, see Candle wax above.

Chocolate & cocoa: First scrape off as much as possible with a dull knife. Hot soapy water will then remove fresh stains from washable articles. If a brown stain remains, use gall soap followed by a good rinse in warm water, or soak in EM. For non-washable materials, dampen the dry fabric stain with cleaning water (see p. 210) and remove with a good fibre cloth. Repeat until all particles are removed.

Chutney: See Tomato juice, relish or chutney.

Cod liver oil: Fresh stains can be removed successfully by washing in warm water and gall soap. Stubborn stains on all fabrics respond to soaking overnight in gall soap or soda. Old stains set by washing and ironing, and are almost impossible to remove, even with bleach.

Coffee & tea: Remove fresh stains from cotton and linen materials by first rinsing in warm water then pouring boiling water from a height of 60–100 cm (2–3 feet) onto the stain. Follow by washing in soapy water. If a trace remains, bleach in the sun, or use Panama tree extract or EM.

Correction fluid: Use concentrated Spray & Wipe on the stain. Most Spray & Wipe formulas contain a solvent which will dissolve the liquid paper. Or try a little gasoline (petrol) on the stain, with some good absorbent paper or old cloth behind it. Then use some gall soap to wash out the gasoline. Alternatively, use xylene or toluene (some of the solvents used in making correction fluid). Use like gasoline. Always test an inconspicuous piece of material before proceeding.

Crayons: Dampen with cleaning water (see p. 210) and remove with a good fibre cloth. This almost always works. If not, treat as for candle wax. On wallpaper, after scraping, cover with blotting or brown paper, iron with warm iron, shifting paper repeatedly. Final traces may be covered with a paste of corn flour and cleaning fluid. Allow to dry and brush off. Repeat if necessary.

Deodorants & antiperspirants: Soak in water and EM. Antiperspirants may cause fabric damage and colour damage in some dyes. Colour may be restored by sponging with ammonia. Dilute ammonia with an equal volume of water for use on wool or silk. Rinse well.

Dyes & running colours: These are difficult to remove and no single treatment is successful in all cases. Immediate copious rinsing in tepid water, forcing the water through the stain, is sometimes effective. Washing and sunning will gradually bring results in some cases. Equal parts of methylated spirits (denatured alcohol) and ammonia may also succeed. Use hydrogen peroxide for silk, wool and delicate fabrics.

Egg: Scrape away as much as possible. Soak in EM with lukewarm water. Never use hot water, as heat hardens the stain. Give it some time. If this does not succeed, spread the stain with a paste of cream of tartar and water, adding a crushed aspirin to the paste. Leave for 20–30 minutes. Rinse well in warm water

Fruit juices & berries: Fresh stains are easy to remove, but once dry, they are very obstinate. Treat with cool water first then soak in EM or use Panama tree extract.

Glues, gums & cellulose adhesives: Soaking in cool water will remove water-soluble glues. For waterproof varieties, use spirit solvent, like methylated spirits (denatured alcohol) or amyl acetate. Test before using on synthetic fabrics. Artificial nail glue can be removed using acetone (test on an inconspicuous area first). Acetone evaporates quickly, so hold a wad of absorbent paper or soft cloth against the glue, and soak the acetone through from the other side. (The glue soaks on to the wad of absorbent paper.)

Grass & foliage: Soak in EM and wash, or sponge with methylated spirits (denatured alcohol). Remove this with warm water and where possible wash the article using laundry powder or liquid.

Ice cream, milk & cream: For washable materials, first sponge with lukewarm water, then wash as usual. If the material is not washable, sponge with dry-cleaning fluid, then with cold water.

Indelible pen or pencil: Do not use water as this spreads the stain. Sponge over a pad of soft cloth, using equal quantities of methylated spirits (denatured alcohol) and household ammonia (test coloured fabrics first). Should the colours run, try methylated spirits (denatured alcohol) alone. Rinse or sponge with warm water.

Ink: Dab with buttermilk, rinse with warm water and a bit of ammonia.

Because inks differ in composition it is impossible to find removers that are work for all types of ink spots. The following is a range of suggestions from which you can choose.

❋ Dry the stained area. Mix together 3 parts dishwashing liquid with 1 part of d'Limonene. Soak the stained area in this solution for 10–15 minutes, and then rinse in water as hot as suitable for the fabric. Then wash as usual, but preferably with a laundry liquid. Repeat if necessary.

❋ *Ballpoint pen ink:* First, saturate material with an alcohol-based hair spray (this seems to be a popular method). The alcohol content in the hair spray will break up the ink. Be sure to place an absorbent paper towel or rag under the stain to catch the excess. Then blot the stain with a rag. Repeat the process until the stain is removed, then launder as usual. Test an inconspicuous area first, as some fabrics may be damaged by the hair spray solution. If in doubt, consult with a professional dry cleaner.

❋ *Water based inks:* Try an all-purpose cleaner instead of hair spray. Be sure to place an absorbent paper towel or rag under the stain to catch the excess. Then blot the stain with a rag. Repeat the process until the stain is removed, then launder as usual. Test an inconspicuous area first, as some fabrics may be damaged by the cleaning solution. If in doubt, consult with a professional dry cleaner.

❋ *If the stain is still wet,* apply an absorbent – French chalk, talcum powder, starch or salt – to absorb excess ink and stop it from spreading. Continue this treatment, removing the discoloured powder and applying fresh, until there no further change is achieved. Alternatively, take up excess ink with blotting paper, pressing fresh patches of blotter into the stain until it no longer discolours. Then treat as required.

❋ *For dried writing ink, ball point pen, or marking ink* soak the stain in sour milk – this is an old fashioned, but effective method. Fresh milk also works, but sour milk is faster. Sponge or dip the stain in equal quantities of methylated spirits (denatured alcohol) and household ammonia (test on coloured fabrics first). Rinse in warm water. Rinse again in warm water containing a little ammonia, then finally in fresh water. Sponge with pure Dettol (Lysol). If not effective, try isopropyl alcohol or dry-cleaning fluid (from chemist).

Iodine: Very fresh stains can often be removed by normal washing or by moistening the stain with water and placing in the sun or before a radiator. If not successful, apply a solution of 1 tsp sodium thiosulphate (from chemist) in 1 cup warm water. Rinse well.

Laundry that took on colour: Soak in Epsom Salt and wash again.

Leather: Fresh fatty stains are best removed by rubbing it gently with stiffly beaten egg-white. First try on a hidden area.

Light oils like sewing machine, hair or baby oil. Rub some dishwashing liquid into the stain, leave for 10–15 minutes, then hot wash (60-65°C, 140–150°F) using your normal laundry detergent. Repeat if any stain remains. For non-washable fabrics or articles, see Butter.

Lipstick & other cosmetics like eyeshadow, mascara or blusher. Washing with your usual laundry product may remove these stains. Pre-treat the dry fabric stain with a laundry pre-soak (spot stain remover). On an non-washable fabric, first try dry-cleaning fluid. If stains are stubborn, sponge with equal quantities of methylated spirits (denatured alcohol) and household ammonia. (Test on coloured fabrics first.) If colour fades, reduce ammonia by half and test again. Rinse in warm water, or wash if possible.

Medicines: Try to find out from doctor or chemist what the medicine contains, as this will aid in selecting the correct treatment, for instance, treat iron tonics as for Rust, rinse alcohol-based medicines with methylated spirits (denatured alcohol). Where contents cannot be discovered see Unknown.

Mildew on fabric: Soak overnight in sour milk and dry. Wash as normal without rinsing it first. Treat as soon as discovered, before the mould has time to weaken the cloth. Slight, fresh stains can often be removed by washing with your usual laundry product and drying in the sun. Otherwise, try following methods in turn, proceeding carefully with coloured articles.

a) Chlorinated laundry bleaches may be used for white untreated cottons and linens, according to general instructions given by the manufacturer. Rinse thoroughly before washing.
b) Vinegar added to the final rinse will help remove any traces of smell remaining from the bleach.
c) A diaper wash/sanitiser containing sodium percarbonate is safe on all white and coloured fabrics.

Motor grease & heavy motor oil: Scrape away as much as possible. For washable materials, rub lard or Vaseline (petroleum jelly) into stain, or treat dry fabric with a laundry pre-soak (spot stain remover). Wash in a quality laundry powder or liquid. On non-washable materials, such stains are difficult. Treat repeatedly with dry-cleaning fluid, continuously changing the pad and the sponging cloth. Finish with a sponging of lukewarm water and synthetic detergent, then warm water to rinse. If contaminated with metal particles, an iron stain may remain. Treat as for Rust.

Mud: Allow to dry, then brushing off. Any remaining stain may be removed by washing or sponging with your usual laundry powder or liquid or if greasy dirt, pre-treat dry fabric with a laundry pre-soak (spot stain remover) or use a grease solvent, like dry-cleaning fluid.

Mustard: Scrape any excess mustard from the fabric, ensuring you don't spread the stain any further. Dry the mustard-stained area. Mix together 3 parts dishwashing liquid with 1 part d'Limonene based product. Soak the stained area in this solution for 10–15 minutes. On occasion the mustard stain will turn very dark, but don't panic – it will wash out. After soaking rinse in water as hot as suitable for the fabric, then wash as usual, but preferably with a laundry liquid. Repeat if necessary.

Nail polish: Apply acetone or amyl acetate (polish removers), but take care with synthetic fibres, as both dissolve some types of rayons. Wash or sponge with your usual laundry product after treatment. Remove any remaining colour with a bleach, using a chlorinated laundry bleach for white cottons and linens. Use hydrogen peroxide for wool and silks.

Oil, fat on fabrics: Gall soap or other alkaline soap. Sprinkle with salt, let it sit a bit then wash.

Paint: Modern paints vary greatly in composition and it is not possible to give one treatment for all types. As a guide, use the solvent suggested on the paint tin label for thinning paint and cleaning brushes. Treat promptly, as set stains are very difficult to remove. If paint has dried, soften with glycerine before applying treatment.

For oil paint, enamels and alkyd type paints, scrape off as much as possible and soak remaining stain in turpentine or kerosene. Then wash in usual way.

Latex or plastic water-base paints, (acrylic and PVA) will wash out easily with cold water when fresh. Remove any remaining stain with methylated spirits (denatured alcohol). Test first to see that acetate fabrics are not affected. Once dry, these paints are virtually impossible to remove.

Pencil marks (lead): Try a soft rubber for non-washable garments. Use a quality laundry powder or liquid on lead pencil marks, but never for indelible pencil. If not successful, follow instructions for Indelible pen or pencil.

Perfume: Wet area, apply glycerine and rinse out well, or sponge with equal parts of full-strength hydrogen peroxide and water. If the colour has already been removed from the fabric by the alcohol in the perfume, it may help to add a few drops of methylated spirits (denatured alcohol) to cheesecloth pad and sponge fabric lightly, working towards the centre of the stain, thus distributing remaining colour evenly.

Perspiration: Dissolve a few aspirin in water and soak for a short while. Wash. Older perspiration stains turn alkaline and sponging with 1 tbsp vinegar in ½ cup water will often restore the colour. This treatment also helps to remove perspiration odours. To remove perspiration stains from non-washable garments or for any stubborn marks, apply a paste of 1 tbsp cream of tartar, 3 crushed aspirins and warm water. Leave for 20 minutes. Rinse well in warm water. Repeat if necessary. Follow this with vinegar and water to restore the colour if necessary.

Red wine: Immediately pour lots of salt on, allow to sit for a while, then wash normally. Do the same with carpets, but pour some water over it and carefully dab dry with fibre cloth. Mineral water works even better.

Relish: See Tomato juice, relish or chutney.

Rust: Any of the methods given below are safe for white fabrics, but test on coloured fabrics before use.

- *Lemon juice* – suitable for light stains on delicate fabrics. Spread stain over a bowl of boiling water and sprinkle with lemon juice. After a few minutes, rinse well and repeat if necessary.
- *Lemon juice and salt* – sprinkle stain with salt, rub with lemon juice and place in sunlight. Keep moist with lemon juice until stain goes. Rinse well.
- *Cream of tartar* – for extensive staining, boil in a liquid made from 4 tsp cream of tartar in 600 ml (½ quart) water. Rinse well. If less extensive, dampen stain, spread with cream of tartar, hold in steam from boiling kettle. Rinse immediately stain goes. Do not use on fabrics that cannot be washed in hot water.

Scorch marks are different from a true stain in that the actual fibre is damaged. Severe marks on any fabric, or scorch marks on wool and silk can seldom be restored. Brushing with fine emery paper may improve a scorched woollen surface.

Very light scorch marks can often be removed by immediate washing with your usual laundry product, followed by a day in the sun. Alternatively, sponge with 1 tbsp borax in 1 cup warm water.

Light scorch marks on white materials can be treated with hydrogen peroxide. Dampen a scrap of white cotton cloth with hydrogen peroxide and lay it on the mark. Cover with a clean dry cloth, then press with a medium warm iron. If the peroxide soaks through the top cloth, move to a dry position. Repeat the treatment until the stain is removed. Rinse well in warm water.

Light scorch marks on any fabric may be treated by sponging with diluted hydrogen peroxide to which a few drops of ammonia have been added (test colours first). Rinse well in warm water.

Shiny spots on woollens: Cut a raw potato in half and carefully rub on the spots. Allow to dry in an airy place and brush with clean soft brush.

Shoe creams: Scrape off any excess with a dull knife. Shoe creams can frequently be removed from washable materials by washing with your usual laundry product. If this is not successful, treat washable fabrics with glycerine. Pour on to the stain, rub lightly between the hands, leave for half an hour, then wash or rinse in warm water.

On non-washable fabrics or for very stubborn marks, sponge with equal quantities of methylated spirits (denatured alcohol) and household ammonia. (Test on coloured fabrics first). Then sponge with warm water.

Sock stains: Soak overnight in salt water to remove brown stains.

Soft drinks: Soak in EM or sponge with equal quantities of methylated spirits (denatured alcohol) and water. Old or obstinate stains may be softened in glycerine before treatment as above.

Soot & smoke: First treat with absorbent powder, then wash. For non-washable articles sponge with citrus oil or other grease solvent, followed by airing to remove smell of smoke. For carpets, mix solvent to a paste with corn flour, talcum or French chalk. Apply thickly, leave to dry, then brush or vacuum off. Repeat if necessary. Use absorbent powder only on rubber backed carpeting.

Soy sauce: Dry the soya sauce-stained area. Mix together 3 parts dishwashing liquid with 1 part of a d'Limonene product. Soak the stained area in this solution for 10–15 minutes, and then rinse in water as hot as is suitable for the fabric. Then wash as usual, but preferably with a laundry liquid. Repeat if necessary. This treatment may require repeating.
Tar and car grease: Scrape away as much as possible with a dull knife. Rub with eucalyptus oil, dab with milk, then wash. Or rub a little butter on the stain, rub with a little benzene, wash normally.

For non-washable materials the stain will be very difficult. Sponge repeatedly with dry-cleaning fluid. If the mark still persists, rub with Vaseline (petroleum jelly), leave for half an hour, then dip in dry-cleaning fluid. If possible, finish by sponging with a solution made from a good quality laundry liquid, starting well to the outside of the stain.

Tarnish: Metallic stains from belts, jewellery, etc., sometimes stain clothes. Sponge with vinegar, lemon juice or 10% solution acetic acid (check synthetics first). For tarnished metallic fabrics, e.g. lamé, if practicable, boil in salt water (2 tbsp to 600 ml or ½ quart). Not suitable for plastics. Otherwise, sponge with methylated spirits (denatured alcohol) or dry-cleaning fluid.

Tobacco: For stubborn tobacco stains, first try pouring glycerine over the stain. Rub lightly between the hands, or pre-treat the dry fabric with a laundry pre-soak (spot stain remover), leave for half an hour then wash in the usual way. If this is not successful, use sodium thiosulphate (see Iodine).

Tomato juice, relish or chutney: Soak in EM or sponge thoroughly with cold water first. The pour glycerine over the affected area, rub lightly between the hands and leave for half an hour.

Unknown: If a stain cannot be identified, treat with cool water first, then sponge with a good quality laundry liquid solution. Rinse well and if stain persists try equal quantities of methylated spirits (denatured alcohol) and ammonia, testing first to note effect on colour and fabric. If colour is affected, omit ammonia. As a last resort, try a mild bleach.

Urine: Here EM is very effective. As the stains differ in composition, the same method may not be successful in all cases. Normally urine is acidic. Sponge with a solution of 1 tbsp household ammonia in ½ cup warm water. Rinse well. If this is not successful, try equal quantities of vinegar and warm water in case the stain is alkaline. Rinse well in warm water. For stubborn stains, sponge with diluted hydrogen peroxide, then wash or sponge – rinse with clear warm water. Old stains may destroy the colour of the cloth, and nothing can be done to restore it in this case.

Vomit: Soak in EM first or sponge with warm water containing a little ammonia. If extensive, dampen and sprinkle with pepsin powder, leave half an hour, then rinse off.

Water spots: Some silks, rayons and wools may be stained by water. To remove such spots, hold in the steam from a rapidly boiling kettle. Cover the spout with butter muslin first to prevent any droplets of water reaching the fabric. Allow the fabric to become damp, but not wet. Shake and press while still slightly damp, rubbing, if possible, with a piece of the same or a similar material, or with fingernail or spoon.

Water stains on carpets become brown because of impurities from backing or underfelt. Mop up spills, wipe with cool water, cover with pad of blotting paper, tissues or absorbent cloth. Weight down with books, etc., and dry quickly with the aid of fan heaters, vacuum exhaust, etc. This causes stain to wick through to absorbent material. Repeat if required.

Wine, red: Immediately pour some white wine on the affected area and soak up. Then wash in cold water and ammonia. Treat promptly, trying mild measures first. Then rinse thoroughly.

Wine, white: Wash in cold water and ammonia. If unsuccessful, follow other treatments under Alcohol. Treat promptly, trying mild measures first. Then rinse thoroughly.

Wood sap: Mix 1 part turpentine (enamel paint thinners) and 4 parts dishwashing liquid, and rub into the sap stain. Leave for 20 minutes and then wash in water and your usual laundry detergent as hot as the fabric will allow. You may have to repeat this process.

Notes

CHAPTER 1

1. Murray, *The Scottish Himalayan Expedition*, p. 6.

CHAPTER 2

1. Steiner, Rudolf, *Foundations of Esotericism*, lecture of Oct 11, 1923.
2. Leroi-Gourham, *Hand und Wort*, p. 388.
3. Kaufmann, *Mit Leib und Seele: Theorie der Haushältigkeit*.
4. Woloschin, *The Green Snake*, p. 23.

CHAPTER 3

1. Aïvanhov, Omraam Mikhaël, *Daily Meditations*.
2. Steiner, *Die Mission der neuen Geistesoffenbarung*, lecture of Feb 23, 1911.
3. Steiner, *Theosophy*, p. 158.
4. Steiner, *The Karma of Vocation*, lecture of Nov 12, 1916, pp. 81f.
5. Grimm, *Deutsche Sagen*.
6. Steiner, *The Spiritual Hierarchies*, lecture of April 12, 1909, pp. 22f.
7. Steiner, *The Philosophy of Freedom*, p. 13.
8. Steiner, *Natur und Geistwesen*, lecture of June 9, 1908.
9. Burkhard, *Gute Träume für die Erde*.

CHAPTER 4

1. Steiner, *Spiritual Science as a Foundation for Social Forms*, lecture of Sep 5, 1920, p. 237.
2. Aivanhov, *Daily Meditations 2010* (Aug 19).
3. Steiner, *Man as Symphony of the Creative Word*, lecture of Nov 11, 1923, p. 214.
4. Dieter Zimmermann, born 1948, is an artist who collects objects that have been thrown away, and makes articles and new pieces of furniture.
5. Porz, Elfie, *Putzen als Ausdruck seelischer Prozesse*, thesis at Augsburg University.
6. Horsfield, *Der letzte Dreck*.

CHAPTER 5

1. George Herbert (1593–1633), from *The Temple*.

2. Carmichael, *Carmina Gadelica*, No 82, p. 93.

3. Steiner, *Love and its Meaning in the World*, lecture of Dec 17, 1912, pp. 182f.

4. Steiner, *How to Know Higher Worlds: A Modern Path of Initiation*, Ch. 1, p. 26.

5. Kiel-Hinrichsen, *Warum Kinder trotzen.*

CHAPTER 6

1. Berti, Daniel, *Tagungshandbuch zur Putzfachtagung.*

2. Anonymous verse, found by Charlotte Koch.

3. Interview with Heinrich Jaenecke, *Der Stern*, No. 14, 1980, pp. 306–9.

4. Rosenberg, Marshall B. *Nonviolent Communication.*

CHAPTER 7

1. From Hesse, Hermann, *The Glass Bead Game* (translator unknown).

2. Murray, *The Scottish Himalayan Expedition*, p. 6.

3. Steiner, *The Spiritual Foundation of Morality*, lecture of May 30, 1912, pp. 47f.

4. Bachelard, Gaston, *The Poetics of Space.*

5. Steiner concluded a public lecture about education (Sep 24, 1919) with this verse. Translated by Malcolm Gardner.

6. Bosco, Henri, *Le Jardin d'Hyacinthe*, pp. 192, 173.

7. Aïvanhov, *Daily Meditations.*

8. Zimmermann, *www.dizi.de.*

9. See Sandra Felton's website *www.messie.com.*

10. See *www.veronika-schroeter.de.*

CHAPTER 9

1. Steiner, *The Education of the Child*, p. 22.

2. *Schatzkammer des Lebens: die ersten sieben Jahren des Lebens*, Anthrosana, No 210.

3. Spitzer, *Lernen: Gehirnforschung und die Schule des Lebens*, and Palmer, *Toxic Childhood.*

4. Steiner, *Sprüche, Dichtungen, Mantren. Ergänzungsband.*

5. Williamson, *A Return to Love*, Ch. 7, Section 3, p. 190.

CHAPTER 10

1. Preuschoff, *Gewalt an Schulen.*

CHAPTER 11

1. *www.prweb.com/releases/acidic_ionized_water/chemical_free_ cleaning/prweb10607805.htm*

2. Meyer, Ulrich, 'Verträglichkeit natürlicher ätherischer Öle bei ausgewiesenen Duftstoff-Mix-Allergikern,' *Der Merkurstab*, pp. 61–63, No. 1, 2004. Weleda , 'Natürliche Öle sind gut verträglich,' *Weleda-Nachrichten*, No. 229, 2003.

3. See Stain Guide on *www.chemistry.co.nz*

Bibliography

Aivanhov, Omraam Mikhaël, *Daily Meditations*. Editions Prosveta, France.

Bachelard, Gaston, *The Poetics of Space*, Beacon Press, Boston 1969.

Berti, Daniel, *Tagungshandbuch zur Putzfachtagung*, 2004.

Bosco, Henri, *Le Jardin d'Hyacinthe*.

Burkhard, Ursula, *Gute Träume für die Erde,* Werkgemeinschaft Kunst und Heilpäda-
gogik 1990.

Carmichael, Alexander, *Carmina Gadelica*, Floris Books 1992.

Emoto, Masaru, *The Miracle of Water*, New York 2007.

Grimm, *Deutsche Sagen*. [German legends], Berlin 1816.

Horsfield, Margaret, *Der letzte Dreck*, Frankfurt 1999.

Kaufmann, Jean Claude, *Mit Leib und Seele: Theorie der Haushältigkeit*, Konstanz 1999.

Gibran, Khalil, *The Prophet*.

Kiel-Hinrichsen, Monika, *Warum Kinder trotzen*, Stuttgart 1999.

Leroi-Gourham, A. *Hand und Wort. Die Evolution von Technik, Sprache und Kunst,*
Frankfurt 1987.

Murray, William Hutchison, *The Scottish Himalayan Expedition*, 1951.

Palmer, Sue, *Toxic Childhood: how modern life is damaging our children and what we can
do about it*. Orion 2006.

Paraselsus, *Liber de Nymphis, Sylphis, Pygmaeis et Salamandris et de Caeteris Spiritibus.*
Published in German as *Das Buch von den Nymphen, Sylphen, Pygmaeen und Sala-
mandern und den übrigen Geistern,* Marburg 1996.

Preuschoff, Gisela and Axel, *Gewalt an Schulen, und was dagegen zu tun ist,* Cologne
1997.

Rosenberg, Marshall B. *Nonviolent Communication: a Language of Life*, PuddleDancer
Press, USA 2003.

Schmidt Brabant, Manfred, *The Spiritual Task of the Homemaker*, Steinerbooks, USA
1999.

Spitzer, Manfred, *Lernen: Gehirnforschung und die Schule des Lebens*, Heidelberg 2002.

Steiner, Rudolf. Volume Nos refer to the Collected Works (CW), or to the German
Gesamtausgabe (GA).

—, *The Education of the Child*, Anthroposophic Press, USA 1996.

—, *Foundations of Esotericism* (CW 93a) Rudolf Steiner Press, UK 1983.

—, *How to Know Higher Worlds: A Modern Path of Initiation* (CW 10) Anthroposophic Press, USA 1994.

—, *How to Cure Nervousness* (part of GA 143), Rudolf Steiner Press, UK 2008.

—, *The Karma of Vocation* (CW 172) Anthroposophic Press, USA 1984.

—, *Love and its Meaning in the World* (CW 143) Anthroposophic Press, USA 1998.

—, *Man as Symphony of the Creative Word* (CW 230) Rudolf Steiner Press, UK 1970.

—, *Die Mission der neuen Geistesoffenbarung* (GA 127) Dornach 1975.

—, *Natur und Geistwesen: Ihr Wirken in unserer sichtbaren Welt* (GA 98) Dornach 1983.

—, *The Philosophy of Freedom* (CW 4) Rudolf Steiner Press, UK 1964.

—, *The Spiritual Foundation of Morality* (part of GA 155) Anthroposophic Press, USA 1995.

—, *The Spiritual Hierarchies and the Physical World* (CW 110) Steinerbooks, USA 2008.

—, *Spiritual Science as a Foundation for Social Forms* (CW 199) Anthroposophic Press, USA 1986.

—, *Sprüche, Dichtungen, Mantren. Ergänzungsband* (GA 40a) Dornach, 2002.

—, *Theosophy* (CW 9) Anthroposophic Press, USA 1994.

Williamson, Marianne, *A Return to Love: Reflections on the Principles of 'A Course in Miracles'*, HarperCollins 1992.

Woloschin, Margarita, *The Green Snake*, Floris Books 2010.

Woodburn, Kim & Mackenzie, Aggie, *How clean is your house?* London 2003.